Going Places 1

Picture-Based English

Teacher's Resource Book

Lois Maharg

Longman

Going Places: Picture   Based English, Teacher's Resource Book 1

Copyright © 1995 by Addison–Wesley Publishing Company, Inc.
All rights reserved.

A Publication of World Language Division

Associated companies:
Longman Group Ltd., London
Longman Cheshire Pty., Melbourne
Longman Paul Pty., Auckland
Copp Clark Pitman, Toronoto

Acquisitions Director: Joanne Dresner
Acquisitions Editor: Anne Boynton-Trigg
Development Editor: Debbie Sistino
Consulting Editor: Michael Rost
Project Manager: Helen B. Ambrosio
Text Design Adaptation: Pencil Point Studio

ISBN: 0-201-82534-1

1 2 3 4 5 6 7 8 9 10-VG-9998979695

CONTENTS

Introduction

Going Places: Picture-Based English is a complete two-level course for beginning ESL students. It is designed to help students develop the practical language they need to function effectively at work, in the community, and in their personal lives. Going Places 1 consists of a fully illustrated Student Book, classroom audio cassettes, and a Teacher's Resource Book. The Student Book includes 27 units based on a carefully organized syllabus that integrates topical, lifeskill, and grammatical strands. The gradual progression of structural elements combined with the unique presentation of practical vocabulary make Going Places the ideal course for students beginning their study of English. Going Places features:

- pictures *without captions* as a vehicle for introducing and practicing new language

- integration of language structures and functional vocabulary within lifeskill contexts such as shopping, health care, and housing

- development of and practice in the four language skill areas of listening, speaking, reading, and writing, progressing in emphasis from reception to production

- opportunities for meaningful, personalized communication using newly acquired language

- lessons that engage students in pair practice and small-group interaction

- careful recycling of vocabulary and grammar throughout the book

- a broad range of activities that address various learning styles

- a cultural component in every lesson designed to heighten students' cross-cultural awareness.

The Student Book

Each unit in Going Places 1 follows a consistent format and is taught in three stages. The units begin with the presentation of vocabulary. The key to the successful presentation of vocabulary is to create a natural, personal interaction between teacher and students. Specific questions and sample presentations which help create this natural, personal interaction are provided in the Teacher's Notes at the back of the Student Book.

Presentation of vocabulary is followed by conversation practice in which students practice the new vocabulary and key grammatical structures. Much of the conversation practice is personalized, with students sharing information about themselves with partners.

The expansion activities in Going Places 1 help students achieve lifeskill competencies through listening, speaking, reading, and writing practice. They reinforce the grammatical focus of the unit, review and expand the vocabulary, and further personalize the language students have learned.

The Teacher's Resource Book

The Teacher's Resource Book provides step-by-step procedures for key exercises that recur frequently throughout the Student Book. For each unit of the Student Book, the Teacher's Resource Book features:

- detailed teaching suggestions that help teachers introduce new language structures and prepare students to perform tasks successfully

- sample language presentations for introducing the vocabulary

- recommendations for using selected activities to teach basic aspects of pronunciation, intonation, rhythm, and stress

- expansion activities that reinforce the grammar, vocabulary, and lifeskill components of each unit and challenge students to use the new language in less structured contexts

- reproducible grammar exercises.

Procedures For Key Exercises

Presentation of Vocabulary through Pictures

1. Direct students' attention to an overhead transparency of the pictures on the first page of each unit. If an overhead projector is not available, have students look at the first page of the unit—*not* the second page—in their books.

2. For each unit, refer to Activity 1 under Teaching Suggestions in the Teacher's Resource Book, or turn to the Teacher's Notes in the Student Book, and ask students a series of yes/no and choice questions relating to each picture. For example: *Do men wear dresses?; Do we wear coats when it's **hot** or when it's **cold?***

3. Use simple language to ask the questions, and personalize the new vocabulary by asking questions that relate to students' lives.

4. When necessary, do the following to help students understand and answer your questions.
   a. Use pantomime.
   b. Point to clues in the pictures.
   c. Use "give-away" questions. For example: "Is this a *sweater* or a *store*?"
   d. Simply feed students answers. For example: "Who's wearing a *shirt* in this class?... [No answer from students.] Well, is Peter wearing a shirt [touching Peter's shirt]?... Yes, Peter's wearing a shirt. And who else?. . ."

5. Use each new vocabulary item in several questions as you present it. Also, skip around the page and review frequently. For example:
   Which picture has the ____(shoes)____?; Point to the picture of the ____(skirt)____.

6. Have students keep their pencils down and notebooks closed during the presentation to keep their focus on the *oral* interaction. To give students a brief "visual take" on the new vocabulary items, write new words on the chalkboard as they are introduced and then quickly erase them.

Reinforcement of Vocabulary with Written Cues

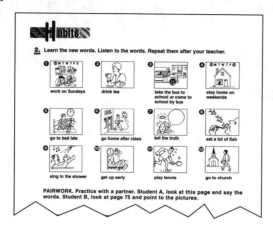

The second page of each unit presents the pictures from the opening page with captions.

1. Model the vocabulary items one by one and have students repeat them.

2. Certain items may require clarification as students are scrutinizing the target vocabulary in print. Answer any questions that arise.

3. Do the pairwork.

   a. First, model the task. Designate yourself as Student A and one of the more capable students as Student B. Have Student B turn to the first page of the unit and hold up his or her book for the rest of the class to see. Hold up your book so that the class sees you're looking at the second page of the unit.

   b. Say the vocabulary items aloud in random order as Student B points to the appropriate pictures, holding up his or her book to show the class.

   c. Put students in pairs, designating one as Student A and the other as Student B. Tell the A's to look at the second page of the unit and the B's to look at the first page. Tell the A's to say the vocabulary items and the B's to point to the appropriate pictures.

   d. As students are doing the pairwork, circulate to make sure they understand the task and to answer any questions.

   e. Have students switch roles for further practice.

Listen and Write

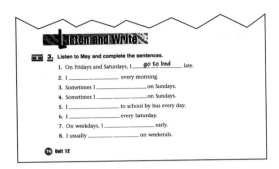

1. Put on the tape and play the instructions and item number 1.

2. Stop the tape. Check to see that students are doing the task correctly by asking what word or phrase they've written in the blank and writing it on the chalkboard. If necessary, play the first item again to verify the accuracy of the response.

3. Continue playing the tape until the end of the exercise. As students listen and write, they may be looking at the words at the top of the page. Do not discourage this. Students cannot be expected to have mastered the spelling of the new vocabulary items yet. If the task is difficult for your class, play the tape a second time.

4. Check students' responses in one of the following ways.

    a. Have individual students read the items aloud, completing the sentences with the words they've written in the blanks. Write the key words on the chalkboard.

    b. Have individual students write the missing words on the chalkboard.

5. Verify the accuracy of students' answers by playing the tape again, stopping it after each item, and asking *Is it right?*

Grammar Box

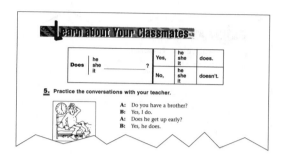

1. Write the material from the grammar box on the chalkboard.

2. Call students' attention to the element of structure being introduced. (This element is often highlighted.) Offer simple explanations of the structural element. For example:

    We use *is* with *he* and *she*.

    We use *are* with *they*.

    Clarify the structures and answer questions as needed, but avoid lengthy explanations.

3. Engage students in an activity that enables them to practice the new structure in an immediate and personalized context. Ideas for such activities are provided in the Teaching Suggestions for each unit.

4. After students have produced a few sentences using the new structure, erase the material from the chalkboard and continue the practice.

Conversation

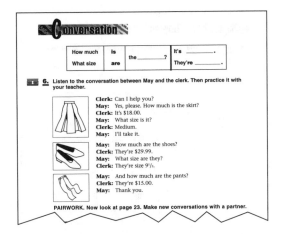

1. If there is a picture next to the conversation, have students look at it and talk about what's happening. Specific questions you may ask to get students to talk about the picture are provided in the Teaching Suggestions for each unit.

2. Some conversations are taped. If the unit has a taped conversation, play the tape.

3. Have students listen as you model the conversation line by line. To indicate when the speaker changes, use dolls or puppets, or turn your body from right to left.

4. Model the conversation a second time and have students repeat it line by line.

5. Have two pairs of students stand up and model the conversation.

6. Tell students to close their books and look at the overhead transparency of the pictures on the first page of the unit. If you don't have an overhead projector, have students turn back to the first page of the unit.

7. Do the pairwork.

   a. First, model the task with one of the more capable students. Point to the first picture on the overhead transparency (or in your book). Ask the appropriate question and wait for the student to answer. Then switch roles: have the student ask you the question.

   b. Have two other students stand up and model the task again. Point to the second picture and have one of the students ask the appropriate question and the other student answer. Then have them switch roles.

   c. Finally, put students in pairs and have them begin the pairwork. Circulate to make sure they understand the task and to answer any questions.

Life Skill/Competency Listening Task

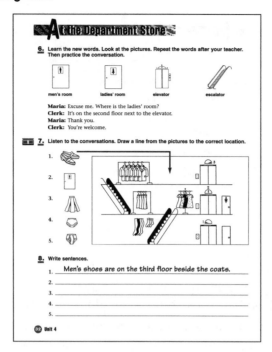

Many units contain listening activities that build students' aural comprehension in life skill and competency areas. The exact nature of these activities varies according to the life skill or competency focus, but all are task based and have the same general format.

1. Prepare students for the listening task by introducing any new vocabulary items that appear at the top of the page. Direct students' attention to the captioned pictures, and have them repeat the new vocabulary items after you. As you introduce each item, ask students yes/no and choice questions. For example, if the vocabulary item is *toothbrush*, ask questions like these: *Michaela, do you use a toothbrush or a comb to clean your teeth?; Is there a toothbrush in your kitchen/bedroom/bathroom?*

2. A dialogue introducing the life skill/competency focus follows the new vocabulary items. If this dialogue is taped, play the tape and then practice it with the class. If not, practice the dialogue with the class as follows.

   a. First, have students listen as you model the dialogue line by line. To indicate when the speaker changes, use dolls or puppets, or turn your body from right to left.

   b. Model the conversation a second time and have students repeat it line by line.

   c. Practice the dialogue again by assuming the role of the first speaker and having the class take the role of the second speaker. Then switch roles.

3. Play the tape and have students listen to the instructions for the task. Then stop the tape and check to see that students have understood by asking them to state in their own words what they're going to do. Whatever the task may be, as students restate the instructions, reinforce them by drawing a circle, a check mark, or a line, or by filling in a blank, on the chalkboard.

4. Continue playing the tape until the end of the exercise. If students are instructed to listen again or if the task is difficult for your class, play the tape a second time.

5. Check students' responses by writing them on the chalkboard as students read them aloud or by having students write them on the chalkboard.

Information Gap

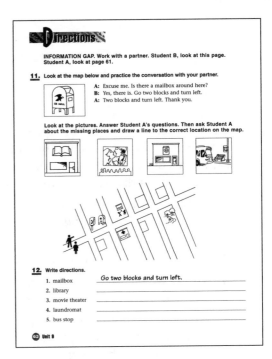

Units 3, 5, 9, 10, and 15 include Information Gap activities.

1. Put students in pairs and designate one as Student A and the other as Student B. Check to see that students know which role they're playing by asking the A's, and then the B's, to raise their hands. Tell the A's to turn to the first page of the Information Gap exercise and the B's to turn to the second page. Have the A's, and then the B's, hold up their books to show they're on the right page.

2. Model any vocabulary items presented at the top of the page and have students repeat them. Then model the short conversations that follow and have students practice them with their partners.

3. Model the Information Gap activity. Designate yourself as Student A and one of the more capable students as Student B, showing the class that the two of you are looking at different pages. Ask Student B for the first piece of information missing on your page, and write down the answer in your book. Hold up your book to show the class the line you've drawn or the information you've written down. Then answer Student B's request for information. If you feel additional guidance is necessary, have two other students model the task again.

4. As students begin to work through the activity with their partners, circulate to make sure they've understood the instructions. There should be no flipping back and forth of pages if students are doing the activity correctly.

5. When students have finished the activity, check their answers by asking the A's and B's for the information missing from their respective pages and writing it on the chalkboard.

6. For more specific instructions as to how to present Information Gap activities, refer to the Teaching Suggestions for each of the five units in which they appear.

Culture Question

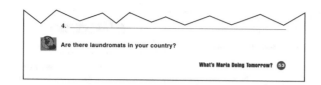

4. _____

Are there laundromats in your country?

What's Maria Doing Tomorrow? 53

Each unit contains a culture question. These culture questions heighten students'
cross-cultural awareness and provide a means for further exploration of the topic or life
skill focus of the unit. All or some of the steps in the following procedure may be used to
stimulate class discussion of the culture question.

1. Have one of the more capable students read the question aloud. For example: _Are
   there laundromats in your country?_ As he or she reads, write the topic (_laundromats_) on
   the chalkboard.

2. Under the topic, make a complete list of students' native countries.

3. Have two or three students from each country (or region) answer the culture question.
   Write the answers beside the appropriate country.

4. Then ask a series of related questions. Yes/no and choice questions are easier to
   respond to than _Wh-_ questions, but all types of questions may be appropriate
   depending on the abilities of individual students. For example, if a student responds in
   the negative to the question _Are there laundromats in your country?_ you may follow up
   with questions like these.

   > _Do some people in your country wash their clothes by hand?;_
   >
   > _Who in the family washes the clothes?; Do they wash the clothes inside or outside the house?_

   If a student responds in the affirmative to the question about laundromats, you may
   follow up with questions like these.

   > _Are laundromats more expensive in your country or in the United States?;_
   >
   > _Are the laundromats in your country in big cities only, or are there laundromats in small
   > towns too?; When are the laundromats open?_

5. As the course progresses, students will become more capable of working in small
   groups. If the culture question lends itself to small group work, for example, _Do many
   people play sports in your country? Which sports are popular?_ you may have students
   interact with their classmates in the following ways.

   a. Have students work with three or four classmates from the same country. In
      response to the culture question about sports, have each group come up with a
      list of sports that are popular in their country. After the lists have been made, have
      group members put their lists on the chalkboard or share their information with
      the rest of the class.

   b. Have students work with three or four classmates from different countries. Ask
      group members to discuss the culture question among themselves, sharing
      information about which sports are popular in their countries.

BEFORE UNIT 1:
English for the Classroom

Topic: the classroom

Life Skills/Competencies: following directions; asking questions in class

Structures: imperatives; plurals

Vocabulary

Listen.	Study Unit 1.	consonants
Look at the chalkboard.	What does this mean?	singular
Write the words.	How do you say this word?	plural
Ask a question.	opposite	right
Answer the question.	How do you spell it?	wrong
Read the sentence.	letters	I don't understand.
Repeat	alphabet	I understand.
Continue. Go on. Next.	vowels	

Teaching Suggestions

Activity 1

This unit is atypical in that the pictures on page 1 (and page 3) are captioned. Present each picture by simply modeling the target sentence and having students repeat.

Activity 2

After students have completed the matching exercise, use the following procedure to practice the sentences and check students' comprehension.

1. Give students TPR* commands and have them respond appropriately. The first time you give the commands, model pantomimed responses for students to imitate. For example:

    Listen to your watch. (Hold your wrist to your ear.)

    Look at the cars outside. (Crane your neck as if looking out the window.)

    Write on the chalkboard. (Write on an imaginary chalkboard in front of you.)

    Read the newspaper. (Hold and page through an imaginary newspaper.)

Have students give pantomimed responses to these commands.

Listen to	your watch.	Look at	your watch.
	the cars outside.		the cars outside.
	the clock.		the clock.
	your neighbor.		your neighbor.
	me.		me.
			your book.
			the chalkboard.

* Total Physical Response is a language learning approach developed by James Asher. It focuses on language acquisition through nonthreatening, physically demonstrated listening comprehension activities.

Write on	your paper.	Read	your book.
	the chalkboard.		the newspaper.
	your desk.		your neighbor's book.
	your hand.		
	your book.		
	your neighbor's desk.		

2. Write the following cues on the chalkboard: *name, day, time, age.* As you point to individual cues, say *Ask the question* or *Answer the question.* For example:

T: (pointing to *name*) Ask the question.

S: What's your name?

T: (pointing to *name*) Answer the question.

S: My name is Thuy.

Do not correct for accuracy. The point of the practice is appropriateness of response.

3. Say one of the following three cues: *1, 2, 3; A, B, C; Monday, Tuesday, Wednesday.* Then follow the cue with one of these commands: *repeat, continue, go on, next.* For example:

T: One, two, three...repeat.

S: One, two, three.

T: One, two, three...continue.

S: Four, five, six.

4. Go back and practice the commands and questions again in random order.

Activity 4

After students have completed the matching exercise, use the following procedure to practice the questions and check students' comprehension.

1. Write these sentences on the chalkboard.

Please look at your book.

Write your name on your paper.

Please repeat the sentence.

Point to individual words or sentences on the chalkboard as you give these commands and ask these questions.

Say the	word.	sentence.	letter.	
How many	words?	sentences?	letters?	
How many vowels in	this word?	the alphabet?		
What's the first	word?	sentence?	letter?	vowel?
What's the last	word?	sentence?	letter?	vowel?

For example:

T: (pointing to *name*) How many vowels?

S: Two.

T: (pointing to *Please look at your book.*) What is the first word?

S: Please.

2. Add the following words to the chalkboard: *up, small, fast, sad, open.* Pantomime the meaning of these words with simple gestures. For example:

Point upward to show the meaning of *up.*

Make a sad face to show the meaning of *sad.*

Open your mouth to show the meaning of *open.*

Now point to individual words on the chalkboard as you ask these questions.

What does this mean? (What's the meaning?); How do you say this?;

How do you spell this? (What's the spelling?); What's the opposite?

For example:

T : (pointing to *up*) What does this mean?

Ss: (pointing upward with fingers)

T: (pointing to *open*) How do you say this?

S: Open.

T: (pointing to *fast*) How do you spell this?

S: F-a-s-t.

T: (pointing to *small*) What's the opposite?

S: Big.

3. Add these words and misspellings to the chalkboard.

book	books	boks
students	student	studetns
renegotiation	interdisciplinary	

Point to individual words on the chalkboard as you ask these questions.

Is this singular or plural?; Is this right or wrong?; Do you understand this?

For example:

T: (pointing to *book*) Singular or plural?

S: Singular.

T: (pointing to *studetns*) Right or wrong?

S: Wrong.

T: (pointing to *renegotiation*) Do you understand?

S: No. I don't understand.

4. Go back and practice the commands and questions again in random order.

UNIT 1 EXERCISES

A. **Match the parts of the sentences.**

1. Ask a   mean?

2. What is the   understand.

3. Look at   1.

4. What does this   this word?

5. How do you   question.

6. Study Unit   the words.

7. I don't   the chalkboard.

8. Write   the sentence.

9. Read   say this word?

10. How do you spell   opposite?

B. **Write the singular form.**

1. boxes	_____	11. children	_____
2. apples	_____	12. classes	_____
3. men	_____	13. people	_____
4. faces	_____	14. dishes	_____
5. buses	_____	15. boys	_____
6. babies	_____	16. feet	_____
7. teeth	_____	17. books	_____
8. hands	_____	18. women	_____
9. inches	_____	19. watches	_____
10. eyes	_____	20. days	_____

Introductions

The main characters that appear throughout the Student Book are introduced on pages 6 and 7.

Page 6

Direct students' attention to the pictures as you read the information at the bottom of the page. Then introduce the four characters by name, pointing to each one and asking these questions.

> *Where is he/she?; What is he/she doing?*

Then point to the characters and have students name them. Finally, ask these questions to check for comprehension.

> *Who's the boss?; Which three people are friends?; Where do they work?*

Page 7

Direct students' attention to the picture as you read the information at the bottom of the page. Then point to John and ask these questions.

> *Who is this?; Where is he?; How many people are in John's family?;*
>
> *Where is John's wife? (Students point to respond.); What's her name?;*
>
> *How many children do John and May have?; What are their names?;*
>
> *Is Tim/Kate/Baby Ben a boy or a girl?*
>
> *Where is Tim/Kate/Baby Ben? (Students point to respond.);*
>
> *Does John's family have a dog?; Where is he? (Students point to respond.);*
>
> *What's his name?*

Review by pointing to the characters and having students name them.

UNIT 1 What's Your First Name?

Topic: personal information

Life Skill/Competency: filling out forms

Structures: *to be*; ordinal numbers

Vocabulary

first name	apartment number	telephone number	year
last name	city	social security number	married
full name	state	age	single
address	zip code	birthday	date
street	area code	month	divorced

Teaching Suggestions
Activity 1

Refer to the procedure on page v.

Present this page by looking at page 10 in the Student Book and asking the questions that appear beside the pictures. (The students will be looking at page 9.) First, ask each question about Maria, whose answers are given on page 9. Then ask the questions of several students, who will give their own answers. The following is a sample presentation of Picture 1 (first/last/full name).

> Today we're going to talk about personal information. Personal information is your name, how old you are, and what else?... your telephone number; and what else?... your address. Those things are all personal information. Let's start with this picture. Do you remember who this is?...It's Maria. And what's this [pointing to her name tag]?...Yes, it's her name. Now, what is her first name?...Good, her first name is Maria. And her last name?...Yes, it's Lopez. Well then, what's her full name?...Right, her full name is Maria Lopez. So what does "full name" mean?...Yes, your full name is your first name and your last name. Now [looking at a student], what's your last name?...Chen? OK. And your first name?...Bao Ping? Yes. So, class, what's his full name?...His full name is Bao Ping Chen.

Activity 2

Refer to the procedure on page vi.

After students finish the pairwork, check their recognition of key terms (e.g., *last name, city, area code*). Hold up flashcards (which you have made before class) with these words and have students read them aloud. Next, go through the flashcards again, and have students first read the word or phrase and then use it in a question that you must answer.

For further reinforcement, refer to Expansion Activity 1.

Activity 5

Give the class additional practice with dates. Write several dates (such as *Sept. 24* or *7/13*) on the chalkboard and have students read them aloud.

Activity 6

Before students begin asking about their classmates' names and birthdays, write these cues on the chalkboard.

first name

spell

birthday

Using these cues, engage several students in a dialogue. For example:

> T: What's your first name?
>
> M: Monica.
>
> T: How do you spell it?
>
> M: M-o-n-i-c-a.
>
> T: When's your birthday?
>
> M: October nineteenth.

Then have students interview each other.

Activity 7

When you ask students about the two characters, write their names on the chalkboard. Then say them aloud, clapping on the stressed syllable of the last name and saying it louder than the other syllables. Draw a large dot above the stressed syllable of the last name to show that it receives the most stress, as follows.

John Phillips   Maria Lopez

Explain to students that when we give our names, we say the family name last and say it louder than our personal name. Model each name again, clapping on the stressed syllable. Have students repeat after you.

After students answer your questions about John and Maria, write *Stan Hill* and *Mr. Morgan* on the chalkboard. Put a dot above the stressed syllable of the last name. Say the names aloud, clapping on the stressed syllable of the last name, and have students repeat. Then ask several students what their names are and write them on the chalkboard with a dot above the stressed syllable of the last name. Engage the class in dialogues, helping students pronounce and stress the names of their classmates correctly. For example:

> T: (pointing) Excuse me. What's your name?
>
> H: Huong Pham.
>
> T: What's her name, class?
>
> Ss: Huong Pham.

In addition, give students more practice with *he, she, his,* and *her*. Have two male and two female students go to the chalkboard and write their names, ages, addresses, phone numbers, social security numbers, birthdays, and birth places. Have them stand next to what they have written as you point to the various words and phrases. Ask the class to make questions with *he, she, his,* and *her* that you can answer. For example:

> T: (pointing to a female student's name)
>
> Ss: What's her name?
>
> T: Olga Ramirez.
>
> T: (pointing to a male student's age)
>
> Ss: How old is he?
>
> T: 43.

Activity 8

Point out that we use *at* before addresses, *on* before streets, and *in* before apartment numbers, cities, and states. After students finish the pairwork, give them additional practice with these three prepositions. Hold up flashcards (which you have made before class) with the words *address, street, apartment number, city,* and *state*. Call on students to offer information about themselves using the correct preposition. Go through the flashcards three or four times.

For further reinforcement, refer to Expansion Activity 2.

Activity 9

Before students begin asking about their classmates' names, telephone numbers, and streets, put these cues on the chalkboard.

> first name
>
> spell
>
> telephone number
>
> street
>
> spell

Model the task by engaging two or three students in dialogues. For example:

T: What's your first name?

R: Regat.

T: How do you spell it?

R: R-e-g-a-t.

T: What's your telephone number?

R: 555-6551.

T: What street do you live on?

R: Divisidero.

T: How do you spell it?

R: D-i-v-i-s-i-d-e-r-o.

Then have students interview each other.

Activity 11

Students may not be familiar with the abbreviations and terms *m.i. (middle initial), sex, M, F, date of birth, place of birth, marital status, widowed, occupation,* and *signature,* so explain their meaning as you go over the form.

Expansion Activities

1. Review personal information questions by playing a modified version of the game Twenty Questions. All students must have their textbooks closed. Divide the class into three teams. One student goes to the front of the classroom. Students on each team take turns asking the student at the front of the room questions (e.g., *What's your name? What's your area code?*) that he or she must answer. Each time a team member asks an appropriate question, his or her team gets a point. You may award points based on grammatical accuracy or comprehensibility. Keep score on the chalkboard. When no one can think of any more questions, the team with the most points wins the game. If you feel students will benefit from additional practice, ask another student to come to the front of the room and play the game again.

2. To review words and phrases relating to personal information, have students number a sheet of notebook paper from one to ten. Say ten of these words or phrases aloud, one by one, having students write information about themselves. For example, when you say *street,* students should write the name of the street they live on. When students have written the ten pieces of information, check their comprehension by having them state this information about themselves in complete sentences. For example: *I live on Washington Street.*

Read the information on the form. Then complete the conversation below.

NAME	*Hill* *Stan*
	(last) (first)
ADDRESS	*1308 Bay St., Apt 20*
	Los Angeles, CA 90118
TELEPHONE *(213) 555-7801*	SOC.SEC. NO. *516-77-9832*
DATE OF BIRTH *3/23/74*	AGE *22*
MARITAL STATUS ☒ single ☐ married ☐ divorced ☐ widowed	

1. A: What's your name?

    B: _____

2. A: What's your address?

    B: _____

3. A: _____

    B: My zip code is 90118.

4. A: What's your telephone number?

    B: _____

5. A: _____

    B: My social security number is 516-77-9832.

6. A: How old are you?

    B: _____

7. A: _____

    B: I was born on March 23, 1974.

8. A: _____

    B: I'm single.

UNIT 2   Where's John?

Topic: places in town
Life Skill/Competency: grocery shopping
Structure: *to be*
Vocabulary

store	airport	party	milk	beans	can
hospital	beach	home	tomatoes	cereal	jar
movie theater	zoo	school	oil	bottle	box
bus stop	park	work	jam		

Teaching Suggestions
Activity 1

Refer to the procedure on page v.

Help students with the pronunciation of the names on this page by modeling them. Have students repeat as necessary. These names reappear throughout the book.

Ask questions like the following to present the pictures.

> Where's this person? (What place is this?)
>
> Is there a ____(park)____ near your house?
>
> Is there a ____(park)____ in our city? Where is it?
>
> What do we do at a ____(park)____?
>
> When do we go to a ____(park)____?
>
> Are you inside or outside when you're at a ____(park)____?

The following is a sample presentation of Picture 1 (at the store).

> Today, we're going to talk about places. First, let's see where John is. See John's name here? Is he at home, or is he at the store?...Yes, he's at the store. Now, what do you do at a store?...You buy food at a store. And what else?...Yes, you can buy clothes at a store. Are there any stores near your house?... There's a drug store near your house, José? Anybody else?...There's a supermarket near your house, Mei. Yes, a supermarket is a store. And where are there lots of stores?...OK, on Main Street. Now take a look at this word [pointing to "sale" in the picture]. It says "sale." Do you know what a sale is?...Well, do you have a sale at a store or at school?...Yes, you have a sale at a store. And what is a sale?...OK, a sale means a cheap price. Is a sale an everyday price?...No, it's a special, cheap price. So where is John?...At the store. And the store is having a sale.

Activity 2

Refer to the procedure on page vi.

Point out that, unlike other vocabulary items, the last three items—*at home, at school,* and *at work*—do not take an article.

Grammar Box   (page 19 of the Student Book)

Refer to the procedure on page viii.

Review the terms *singular* and *plural* and the personal pronouns *he, she,* and *they*. Ask students these personal information questions: *Where are you from? How old are you? Are you married or single?* Then ask the class to report the answers. For example:

T: Juan, where are you from?

J: I'm from Mexico.

T: Class, where is Juan from?

Ss: He's from Mexico.

T: Natalia, where are you from?

N: I'm from Mexico.

T: Class, where are Juan and Natalia from?

Ss: They're from Mexico.

Activity 4

Refer to the procedure on page ix.

As students look at the picture above the conversation, ask these questions.

Is John in this picture?; Where is he?; Are other people at the store?;

Are they happy?; Why not?

Activity 5

Put the two conversations on the chalkboard. As you model each line, ask the students which word is loudest in each question and answer. Mark the primary stress with a dot, as follows.

A: Who's at schŏol?

B: Păblo is.

A: Who's at the ăirport?

B: Mr. and Mrs. Mŏrgan are.

Have students repeat each sentence, stressing the correct word. Then erase the conversations from the chalkboard.

Before students begin the pairwork, give them additional practice with the new structure. Ask them to point to the door, the windows, the chalkboard, and the teacher's desk. Then station individuals and pairs of students at these places and have the class answer your questions, reminding them to stress the name. For example:

T: Who's at the chalkboard?

Ss: Tuan is.

Last, point to the individuals and pairs of students standing around the classroom and have the class ask you questions, reminding them to stress the final noun. For example:

Ss: Who's at the door?

T: Abdullah and Yen are.

Activity 6

Before students do the writing task, review family terms by asking students about members of their family. For example:

Are you married?; What's your husband's name?; Where is he now?

After students finish the writing task, have them share some of their sentences with the class.

Activity 7

Refer to the procedure on page x.

After introducing the food items, check students' comprehension. Put food, food realia, or large pictures of the foods in different places around the classroom. Ask students to point to the items as you say them. Then, hold up the objects or pictures and ask students to name them.

Before listening to the conversation, direct students' attention to the picture of the store. Ask these questions.

What is this?; How many aisles are there in the store?;

Who is John talking to? (the clerk)

Activity 8

When students finish the pairwork, have them take out their notebooks and write complete sentences about the location of the foods. For example: *The milk is on aisle 6.*

Activity 9

Bring in containers or pictures of containers and check students' comprehension as you did in Activity 7.

Activity 11

Put these lists on the chalkboard and model the pronunciation of any foods suggested by the students. You may also bring in realia or pictures of some of the new foods on the following day to reinforce the additional vocabulary.

For reinforcement of foods and containers, refer to Expansion Activities 1, 2, and 3.

Expansion Activities

1. Dictate the names of the foods and the containers on pages 21 and 22 and have students draw pictures of the objects and label them.

2. Using realia, set up a store with foods on different aisles and have students role-play dialogues between a clerk and customers. Before starting the activity, point out that the classroom also has aisles, and put up signs indicating the different aisles in the "store." Ask one student to be the clerk. Then pass out index cards with the names of foods to the other students, who will be the customers. Have the customers engage the clerk in the following dialogue.

   Customer: Excuse me. Where's the oil?

   Clerk: The oil is on aisle 4.

   Customer: Thank you.

   Have the customers walk to the correct aisle and take the food back to their seats.

3. Ask students to visit a local grocery store to gather information about the location and price of the six foods introduced on page 21 of the Student Book. For homework, have them write two sentences about each food. For example:

   The beans are on aisle 5.

   Beans are 89¢ a can.

A. Look at the pictures on page 17. Write the answers.

1. Where's Ann?   _She's at the park._____

2. Who's at the store?   _John is._____

3. Where are Tony and Mark?   _____

4. Where's Pablo?   _____

5. Who's at the beach?   _____

6. Where are Nancy and Matt?   _____

7. Who's at the hospital?   _____

8. Where's Jane?   _____

9. Where are May and Baby Ben?   _____

10. Who's at the airport?   _____

B. Look at the pictures on page 17. Write the questions.

1. _Who's at a party?_____   Nancy and Matt are.

2. _Where's Pablo?_____   He's at school.

3. _____   They're at home.

4. _____   She's at a bus stop.

5. _____   Lee and Peter are.

6. _____   He's at work.

7. _____   Tim and Kate are.

8. _____   They're at the airport.

9. _____   She's at the hospital.

10. _____   Ann is.

UNIT 3 | What Size Is the Shirt?

Topic: clothing items

Life Skill/Competency: clothes shopping

Structure: *to be*

Vocabulary

shirt	ties	hats	dress	yellow	black
blouse	shoes	coat	underwear	green	gray
skirt	socks	jacket	red	blue	brown
sweater	pants	gloves	orange	pink	white
belts	T-shirt				

Teaching Suggestions

Activity 1

Refer to the procedure on page v.

Ask questions like the following to present the pictures.

> What (item of clothing) is this?
>
> How much is this ___(shirt)___?
>
> What size is this ___(shirt)___?
>
> Where (on your body) do you put a ___(shirt)___?
>
> Who in this class is wearing a ___(shirt)___?
>
> What color is his/her ___(shirt)___?

The following is a sample presentation of Picture 1 (a shirt).

> Today we're going to talk about clothes—you know [pointing], shirt, pants, socks: clothes. What's this? Is it a pair of pants?...No. Is it a shirt?...Yes, it's a shirt. Let's see now, who has a shirt on in this class?...Yes, you have a shirt on, Ali. What color is Ali's shirt?...Ali's shirt is blue. Who else?...Yes, Maria has a shirt on. Is that a new shirt or an old one, Maria?...Oh, it's new. It looks new! Now, let's look at the size of this shirt. What size is it [pointing to the "L" in the picture.]?...It's large. What does "large" mean?...Right, it means "big." Anybody here have a large shirt?...Paulo, your shirt size is large? So, class, what does "size" mean?...Yes, it means "big" or "small." Now, what about the price of this shirt? What price is it?...Yes, it's $19.00 [pointing to the price in the picture]. What's the price of this book?...The price was $12.00. And the price of that pencil, Deng?...Oh, the price was 29 cents?

Activity 2

Refer to the procedure on page vi.

After students see and pronounce the new vocabulary items, you may want to introduce these related items: *pocket, sleeves* (*long* and *short*), *button,* and *pair.* Do this by pointing to the examples in the pictures or with clothing students are wearing.

For reinforcement of clothing, refer to Expansion Activity 1.

Activities 3, 4, and 5

As you model the sizes and prices, write a few examples on the chalkboard. In each one, cross out the word *and* and above it write the letter *n,* as follows.

nine $\overset{n}{\text{and}}$ a half   four dollars $\overset{n}{\text{and}}$ fifty cents

three $\overset{n}{\text{and}}$ a half   a hundred $\overset{n}{\text{and}}$ twenty-five dollars

Explain to students that when we say sizes and prices quickly, the word *and* is pronounced as the sound [*n*]. As students repeat the sizes and prices after you, help them reduce the vowel and drop the *d* in *and*.

For more practice with numbers, write additional sizes and prices on the chalkboard and have students read them aloud, reminding them to shorten *and*.

Grammar Box   (page 26 of Student Book)

Refer to the procedure on page viii.

Contrast the pronouns *it* and *they*. First, check students' comprehension of familiar classroom objects by pointing and having students name the objects (e.g., *pen, pencil, book, notebook, desk, table,* and *chair*). Then ask about the location of the objects and have students answer using pronouns. For example:

> T: Where's the book?
>
> Ss: It's on the chair.
>
> T: Where are the pencils?
>
> Ss: They're on the desk.

Activity 6

Refer to the procedure on page ix.

After listening to the conversation, point out that *pants* is always plural and requires a plural verb.

For reinforcement of language related to shopping, refer to Expansion Activity 2.

Activity 7

Before listening to the conversations, review the list of colors in the box. Point to various objects in the classroom and have students say what color they are. Check students' comprehension of colors and clothing, as follows.

First, ask three students to go to the front of the classroom. Ask the other students a series of yes/no questions about the three students' clothing. For example: *Is Cammi wearing a pink sweater? Is Nguyen wearing black pants?* Then have the students return to their seats.

Next, ask a series of *who* questions. For example: *Who's wearing a brown belt?* Have students raise their hands if they're wearing the item you describe.

Activity 8

Information Gap. Refer to the procedure on page xi. Since this is the first Information Gap activity in the book, spend considerable time preparing students to perform the task successfully.

When students have finished the Information Gap activity, ask the A's for information about the men's clothing and the B's for information about the women's clothing and write it on the chalkboard.

For further reinforcement, refer to Expansion Activity 3.

Expansion Activities

1. To review clothing items, have the class make two lists of clothing on the chalkboard—one for men's clothing, and the other for women's clothing. Ask students what men and women wear in their native countries. For example: Do women wear T-shirts in Vietnam? Do men wear hats in Guatemala?

2. Using realia, set up a clothing store and have students role-play dialogues between a salesclerk and customers. First, put this model conversation on the chalkboard and practice it with the students.

Salesclerk: Can I help you?

Customer: Yes, please. How much is the blouse?

Salesclerk: It's $20.00.

Customer: What size is it?

Salesclerk: It's size 10.

Customer: I'll take it.

Erase the model conversation. Then have pairs of students come to the front of the classroom and ask and answer questions about the various items of clothing at the store. Have the "customers" take the clothes they buy back to their seats.

3. Clip and photocopy (or make a transparency of) some clothing advertisements from your local newspaper. Ask students questions about price, size, and color, or have them ask and answer questions working in pairs.

UNIT 3 EXERCISES

A. Read the questions. Write answers about your clothes.

Example: What size is your jacket?   _My jacket is medium._

What color is it?   _It's gray._

1. What size is your shirt?   _____

What color is it?   _____

2. What size are your shoes?   _____

What color are they?   _____

3. What size are your pants?   _____

What color are they?   _____

B. Look at the pictures. Then look at the answers and write the questions.

1.   _How much is the blouse?_ _____   It's $26.00.

2.   _____   It's size 9.

3.   _____   They're dark blue.

4.   _____   They're $12.95.

5.   _____   Extra large.

UNIT 4 Where's Zabu?

Topic: locations

Life Skills/Competencies: department store shopping; kitchen items

Structure: prepositions of location

Vocabulary

inside	on top of	spoon	glass
outside	at the corner	knife	cup
in the corner	next to/beside	fork	pot
around	between	sponge	pan
over/above	men's room	counter	circle
under/below	ladies' room	shelf	square
in front of	elevator	dish	triangle
in back of/behind	escalator	bowl	

Teaching Suggestions

Activity 1

Refer to the procedure on page v.

During the presentation and conversation practice in this unit, students will be asked a question whose answer is not given in the book: *Why is Zabu in this place?* Here, as in other places indicated in the book, the aim is to reinforce the new language (and have some fun) by engaging in free speculation.

For each picture, ask these questions.

Where is Zabu?; Why is he there? (What's he doing there?)

Then elicit other visible illustrations of the preposition being taught, as in the following sample presentation of Picture 1 (inside his house).

> Let's see, who do we have here?...Yes, this is Zabu. And where is he, at home or in the park?...Yes, he's at home. This is his house. Now, is Zabu inside his house or outside his house?...Yes, he's inside his house. "Inside" is the same meaning as...Yes, it's the same as "in." Now, what's Zabu doing inside his house? Any ideas?...Yes, he's just sitting there. Why is he sitting inside his house?...Yes, he looks sad. What is he thinking about?...Maybe he's thinking about food. Now, what about us? Are we inside our houses?...No, we're inside the classroom. And what about my teeth [showing teeth]? They're inside my...yes, inside my mouth. And your money?...Yes, it's inside your purse.

Activity 2

Refer to the procedure on page vi.

Introduce the concept of stress and rhythm in the pronunciation of these prepositional phrases. First, put the phrases on the chalkboard with dots above the stressed syllables. For example:

>   •   •   • •   •   •
> over his house   on top of his house   around his house

Model each phrase for the students. Then clap the rhythm, clapping hard on the stressed syllables, and softly and quickly on the unstressed syllables. For example, after you say the phrase *over his house*, clap hard on *o-* and *house*, and clap softly and quickly on *-ver* and *his*. Have the students first clap the rhythm and then repeat the phrase. Then go through the phrases again, pointing to each one and having students first clap the rhythm and then say the phrase aloud. When you finish, erase the phrases from the chalkboard.

Before students begin the pairwork, give them practice with the prepositions. Ask about the location of objects in the classroom—the door, the windows, chairs, tables, desks, the wastebasket, books, and so on. You may need to move some of these objects around in order to reinforce all of the prepositions.

For further reinforcement, refer to Expansion Activity 1.

Activity 3

Before listening to the tape, check students' comprehension of the vocabulary items by drawing the three shapes on the chalkboard and numbering them 1, 2, and 3. Say the names of the shapes and have students say the corresponding numbers. Then do a dictation in which students must draw the shapes in the order you say them.

Grammar Box   (page 31 of Student Book)

Refer to the procedure on page viii.

Give students practice with short answers by positioning individual students at different places around the classroom and asking yes/no questions about where each one is.

Activities 6, 7, and 8

Refer to the procedure on page x.

For further reinforcement, refer to Expansion Activity 2.

Activity 9

For each of the items on the shelves and counter, ask questions like the following.

> *What's this (called)? (What are these called?)*
>
> *What's it (used) for? (What are they used for?)*
>
> *Where (in the picture) is it? (Where are they?)*

The following is a sample presentation of dishes, knife, and forks.

> What kind of store is this, class? A drug store?...No; it's a department store. But what's all this [pointing]? It looks like a...yes, a kitchen. This woman is cooking food to show the customers. Now look at the things in this kitchen. What are these?...Yes, they're dishes. What are dishes for [pantomiming]?...For eating food. What color are the dishes in your house, Tam?...Your dishes are white. And yours, Yukiko?... Blue. Now, *where* are the dishes—on the floor or on the counter?...Yes, they're on the counter. Do you have a counter in your house, Juan?...Yes, in the kitchen. And are there counters in stores?...Yes, there are. So, these two dishes are on the counter. And what's this?...Yes, it's a knife. What's a knife for [pantomiming]?...For cutting. And where is this knife?...Yes, it's *between* the dishes. What about these?...Yes, they're forks. Do you use forks in China, Jimmy?...Not very much. And where are the forks?...Yes, they're *on top of* the dishes.

Activity 10

Before students begin the pairwork, have them practice the prepositions of location with kitchen objects. Have students follow instructions like these.

> Tomiko, please put the pan in the corner.
>
> Manuel, please put the pot under the chair.

Grammar Box   (page 34 of Student Book)

Refer to the procedure on page viii.

Give students practice with short answers by asking yes/no questions about classroom and kitchen objects. For example:

> T: Is the clock above the chalkboard?
>
> Ss: Yes, it is.

T: Are the forks beside the sponge?

Ss: No, they aren't.

For further reinforcement of dinnerware and prepositions, refer to Expansion Activities 3, 4, and 5.

Expansion Activities

1. Make a list of classroom objects on the chalkboard and have students write full sentences, using prepositions, about the location of these objects. For example:

   The teacher's desk is in front of the class.

   The clock is above the door.

   The table is in the corner of the room.

   Chalkboard computer
   T.V. world map
   bookshelves sink
   books

2. Have students work in small groups or as a class to make lists of merchandise they could buy in a department store. Then ask them to visit their local department store to find the location of these things. For homework, have them write sentences about ten of the items. For example:

   Women's coats are on the third floor beside the dresses.

   The men's room is on the second floor behind the escalator.

3. After students complete the pairwork for Activity 10, give a dictation in which you instruct students to draw kitchen objects in specific locations. Give instructions like these.

   Draw a counter.

   Draw two bowls on the counter.

   Draw a spoon between the bowls.

4. Ask students to bring in utensils, dishware, and cookware commonly used in their native countries and teach the vocabulary for these objects.

5. Ask students to draw a table set for one person as it would appear in their native countries. When they've finished, ask one student to instruct the others in how to draw a place setting in his or her country. After checking students' drawings for accuracy, put the students in pairs (if possible, partners should be from different countries, or at least from different regions of a country). Have them instruct each other in how to draw place settings and compare drawings after they've finished.

UNIT 4 EXERCISES

A. **Look at the picture on page 33. Write the missing words.**

1. Where _____*is*_____ the knife? It's _____*between*_____ the plates.

2. Where _____ the forks? They're _____ the plates.

3. Where _____ the shelf? It's _____ the counter.

4. Where _____ the cereal? It's _____ the pot.

5. Where _____ the glasses? They're _____ the shelf.

6. Where _____ the sponge? It's _____ the bowl.

7. Where _____ the pots? They're _____ the shelf.

8. Where _____ the spoon? It's _____ the bowl.

9. Where _____ the jam? It's _____ the plate.

10. Where _____ the oil? It's _____ the glasses.

11. Where _____ the cups? They're _____ the cans.

12. Where _____ the pan? It's _____ the pots.

B. **Look at the picture on page 32. Write the answers.**

1. Where are women's pants?

   They're on the second floor in front of the escalator.

2. Where are men's coats?

   _____

3. Where is the ladies' room?

   _____

4. Where are the socks?

   _____

5. Where are women's dresses?

   _____

UNIT 5 — What's John Doing?

Topic: activities in town

Life Skill/Competency: school facilities

Structure: present continuous

Vocabulary

school—teach a lesson	hospital—visit a friend	party—dance
home—sleep	park—run	hall
theater—watch a movie	store—buy food	office
bus stop—wait for the bus	zoo—look at animals	listening lab
airport—meet a friend	work—drive a truck	restroom
beach—swim		

Teaching Suggestions

Activity 1

Refer to the procedure on page v.

Ask questions like the following to present the pictures.

Where's this person? (What place is this?)

What's he/she doing?

Is he/she __(sleeping)__ or __(swimming)__?

When do we __(swim)__?

Where do we __(swim)__?

Do you ever __(swim)__?

Do you like to __(swim)__?

The following is a sample presentation of Picture 1 (teach a lesson).

> Today we're going to talk about what people are doing. For example, what are you doing? Are you eating, or are you studying?...You're studying. Now let's see what some other people are doing. First, we have John again. Do you remember where John is in this picture?...Yes, he's at school. And what's he doing? Is he studying?...No, he's not studying. Well, then, is he eating dinner or is he teaching a lesson?...Yes, he's teaching a lesson. Now, who's teaching a lesson in our class? Are you teaching a lesson?...No, you're studying. So who's teaching a lesson?...Yes, I'm teaching a lesson. Is this an English lesson or a cooking lesson?...It's an English lesson. And what lesson am I teaching [pointing to a few of the pictures]? Is it a lesson about clothes?...No, it isn't a lesson about clothes. What lesson am I teaching? It's a lesson about...Yes, a lesson about places.

Grammar Box   (page 37 of Student Book, top)

Refer to the procedure on page viii.

Review the stress pattern in *Who* questions and answers and introduce the concept of falling intonation. First, ask five students to stand in front of the class. Next, ask who's wearing various items of clothing and have the class respond. Write the first three questions and answers on the chalkboard and ask students which word is the loudest in each sentence. Mark the primary stress with a dot. Then model the questions and answers a second time and ask students whether your voice goes up or down at the end of each sentence. Indicate falling intonation with a downward arrow, as follows.

Q: Who's wearing a white shirt?   A: Thuy is.

Q: Who's wearing brown pants?   A: Bao Chu is.

Q: Who's wearing a green jacket?   A: Naomi is.

Have students answer several questions, using the correct stress and intonation pattern in their responses. Then have individual students ask and answer the questions. Help them with stress and intonation.

Activity 4

Refer to the procedure on page ix.

As students look at the picture on the right, ask these questions.

How many people are in this picture?; Where are they?;

What are they doing?; What are they looking at?

Grammar Box   (page 37 of Student Book, middle)

Refer to the procedure on page viii.

Have students practice the structure using verb phrases they're already familiar with. Tell individual students to perform these actions.

Go to the chalkboard.

Write the date.

Draw a circle.

Say the alphabet.

Read the sentence.

As each action is performed, ask the class what each student is doing. For example:

T: Ismael, please go to the chalkboard.... Class, what's he doing?

Ss: Going to the chalkboard.

T: Ismael, please write the date.... Class, what's he doing?

Ss: Writing the date.

After you've done this a number of times, continue giving the commands but have individual students ask and answer the questions.

Activity 5

Refer to the procedure on page ix.

For reinforcement of the verbs presented in this unit, refer to Expansion Activity 1.

Activity 6

For reinforcement of the spelling of -*ing* forms of verbs, refer to Expansion Activity 2.

Activity 7

Before practicing the conversations, do a quick review of family terms. Ask students to generate a list and write it on the chalkboard.

After students complete the pairwork, have them share something they have learned about their classmates' families with the class.

Activity 8

Before students begin the writing task, ask two or three students to talk about what various members of their families are doing now. When students have finished writing, have them share some of their sentences with the class.

Activities 9, 10, and 11

Information Gap. Refer to the procedure on page xi.

As you introduce the new vocabulary words, direct students' attention to the picture of the school. Point out that, in addition to the hall, the office, the listening lab, and the restroom, there are three classrooms in the picture. Then ask students about the location of the rooms. For example:

> T: Where's the listening lab?
>
> Ss: It's next to the office.
>
> T: Where's room 101?
>
> Ss: It's between room 100 and room 102.

To model the Information Gap task, ask Student B where Mark is and what he's doing. On the chalkboard, show students how to draw a line from Mark's name to the hall and how to write what he's doing in Activity 11.

After students have finished the Information Gap activity, ask the A's for information about Mark, Sue, and Ann, and the B's for information about Maria, Lee, and Zabu, and write it on the chalkboard.

For reinforcement and expansion of school-related vocabulary, refer to Expansion Activities 3 and 4.

Expansion Activities

1. Hand each student a flashcard (which you have made before class) with one of the verb phrases from page 36 of the Student Book on it. Have individuals and pairs of students mime their actions in front of the class. Have half of the class ask the question (e.g., *What's he/she doing? What're they doing?*) and the other half respond (e.g., *Buying food*). Then have the students switch roles.

2. To give students additional practice spelling the *-ing* form of verbs, first dictate the simple form of the verbs on page 36 of the Student Book. (If you include *visit*, you'll have to explain that the final *-t* is not doubled in verbs of more than one syllable unless the stress falls on the final syllable of the verb.) Then have students write the *-ing* form.

3. Take the students on a tour of your school building, stopping to note the numbers of the classrooms and the location of the restrooms, offices, and labs. If your school contains rooms for special purposes, such as a computer lab or a teachers' lounge, you can hold up signs with the names of these rooms if they're unmarked.

4. Have students draw a schematic floor plan of the floor where their classroom is located, similar to the picture on pages 39 and 40 of the Student Book. Have students label all the rooms. Then ask location questions and have students respond with sentences containing prepositions. For example:

   > T: Where's the men's restroom?
   >
   > Ss: It's in the corner next to room 274.

   You may also have students ask and answer similar questions in pairs.

UNIT 5 EXERCISES

Look at the pictures on page 35. Write the missing words.

1. Maria is at _____the_____ _____hospital_____ .

   She _____is_____ _____visiting_____ a friend.

2. Tom and Sue are at _____ _____ .

   They _____ _____ food.

3. Baby Ben is at _____.

   He _____ _____ .

4. Ann is at _____ _____ .

   She _____ _____ .

5. Tim and Kate are at _____ _____ .

   They _____ _____ at the animals.

6. John is at _____.

   He _____ _____ a lesson.

7. Tony and Mark are at _____ _____ .

   They _____ _____ a movie.

8. Pablo is at _____.

   He _____ _____ a truck.

9. Nancy and Matt are at _____ _____ .

   They _____ _____ .

10. Lee and Peter are at _____ _____ .

    They _____ _____ .

11. Jane is at _____ _____ _____ .

    She _____ _____ for the bus.

12. Mr. and Mrs. Morgan are at _____ _____ .

    They _____ _____ a friend.

 # Who's Cleaning the House?

Topic: activities at home

Life Skill/Competency: talking about family

Structure: present continuous

Vocabulary
clean the house	cook a meal	get dressed	take a shower
sleep	fill out a form	get undressed	take a bath
wash the dishes	write a letter	drink coffee	not do anything

Teaching Suggestions
Activity 1

Refer to the procedure on page v.

Ask questions like the following to present the pictures.

What's this person doing?

Is he/she __(cleaning)__ or __(sleeping)__ ?

When do we ___(clean)___ ?

Where do we ___(clean)___ ?

Why do we ___(clean)___ ? (Why is he/she ___cleaning___ ?)

Do you like to ___(clean)___ ?

The following is a sample presentation of Picture 1 (clean the house).

> Today we're going to talk again about what people are doing. Who's in this picture?...Yes, it's John. And what's he doing here? Is he teaching a lesson in this picture?...No, he's not teaching a lesson. So what's he doing?...Yes, he's cleaning. And what is he cleaning — his school or his house?...Yes, he's cleaning his house. Now what about you, Phuong, do you clean your house sometimes?...Yes, you do? And do you like to clean your house?...No, you don't like to clean your house. Me neither! I don't like to clean my house. When do you usually clean your house, Phuong? At night? On the weekends?...Oh, you usually clean your house on Sunday. What about you, Leticia, when do you clean your house?... What?? You don't clean your house?!...Oh, I see! Your husband cleans your house. Lucky you!

Activity 3

Refer to the procedure on page vii.

After students complete the Listen and Write activity, review the stress and intonation pattern for *Who* questions and answers. Have students mark the stress and intonation of each of the six questions and answers in their books with a dot above the syllable receiving the primary stress and a falling arrow at the end of the questions and answers. Have them practice this pattern by reading the questions and answers aloud. Encourage and help them to use the correct stress and intonation when they do the pairwork.

Grammar Box   (page 43 of Student Book)

Refer to the procedure on page viii.

Have students practice the structure orally. Bring in six large pictures of individuals and pairs or groups of people performing actions that students can talk about. (You can use newspaper or magazine ads.) Use the pictures and prompts to generate sentences. For example:

T:	(holding up a picture of a sleeping boy) Swim.
Ss:	He isn't swimming.
T:	Read.
Ss:	He isn't reading.
T:	Sleep.
Ss:	He's sleeping.

Activity 5

After students finish the pairwork, have them write complete sentences about what people are doing in the pictures on page 41 of the Student Book.

For review and reinforcement of the verb phrases introduced in Units 5 and 6, refer to Expansion Activities 1 and 2.

Grammar Box (page 44 of Student Book)

Refer to the procedure on page viii.

Introduce the stress and intonation pattern for yes/no questions and short answers. Ask five students to go to the front of the classroom. Ask the rest of the class questions about their clothes. Write some of these questions and answers on the chalkboard. Model the sentences and ask students which word is the loudest in each one. Mark the primary stress with a dot. Then model the sentences a second time and ask students whether your voice goes up or down. Establish the rising intonation pattern for yes/no questions and the rising/falling intonation pattern for short answers by drawing arrows, as follows.

T:	Are Jimmy and Raul wearing blue pants?
Ss:	Yes, they are.
T:	Are they wearing red hats?
Ss:	No, they aren't.

Have students answer several questions, using the correct stress and intonation pattern in their responses. Then have individual students ask and answer the questions. Help them with stress and intonation.

To make the activity more challenging, include the words *sleeves*, *buttons*, and *pocket* in your questions. For example:

T:	Is Ahn wearing a blouse with short sleeves?
Ss:	No, she isn't.

After students have answered several of your questions, have individuals ask and answer the questions, reminding them to use the correct stress and intonation.

Activity 6

Refer to the procedure on page ix.

As students look at the large picture to the right of the conversation, ask these questions.

How many people are in this picture?; Are they men or women?;

Where are they?; What are they doing? Why?; Are they having a good time?

Expansion Activities

1. Review the verb phrases introduced in Units 5 and 6. Ask groups of five or six students to go to the front of the classroom. Hand individuals and pairs of these students a flashcard (which you have made before class) with one of the verbs. Ask the students to mime their actions simultaneously. Then ask *Who* questions. For example:

   T: Who's dancing?

   Ss: Vinh is.

   T: Who's washing the dishes?

   Ss: Lee and Huong are.

   Have the students continue miming their actions. As you point to various individuals and pairs, have the students who are seated make questions and answers. First, have the female students ask the questions and the male students give the answers. Then have the students switch roles.

2. To review familiar verbs and their *-ing* spellings, have the class play Verb Bingo. (The only thing you'll need to prepare is lots of little paper squares or counters or coins that students can use to cover up the squares on their bingo cards, which they will make in class.)

   Have each student draw a grid that is five squares across and five squares down. Then dictate the following list of verbs, instructing students to write a verb in each square. It's important for students to understand that they are not to write the verbs in any particular order, since no two bingo cards should look the same. You may need to demonstrate how to do this by drawing two sample bingo cards on the chalkboard.

looking	writing	asking	reading	studying
saying	spelling	teaching	sleeping	watching
waiting	meeting	swimming	running	buying
driving	dancing	living	taking	stopping
sitting	cleaning	washing	cooking	drinking

   When the bingo cards are finished, begin the game. Call out the verbs in a different order. The first student to get five verbs in a row or on the diagonal wins the game. Prizes may be awarded, but you may want to make receiving them contingent on students spelling all five verbs correctly. The game may be played several times. For a slower group of students, the game may be more manageable if you have them play with a partner, with one bingo card for each pair of students.

A. Look at the pictures on page 41. Read the sentences and write *right* or *wrong*. Then correct the sentences that are wrong.

Examples: Maria is filling out a form.   _right_

_____

Tony is taking a shower.   _wrong_
Tony isn't taking a shower. He's taking a bath.

1.   Stan is washing the dishes.   _____

_____

2.   Nancy and Matt are sleeping.   _____

_____

3.   Peter is drinking milk.   _____

_____

4.   Tom and Sue are cleaning the house.   _____

_____

5.   Ann is writing a letter.   _____

_____

B. Answer questions about your family. Write short answers.

Examples: Is your wife working now?   _No, she isn't._

Are your children living in the United States?   _Yes, they are._

Is your brother studying English?   _I don't have a brother._

1.   Is your father sleeping now?   _____

2.   Are your children studying now?   _____

3.   Is your husband working now?   _____

4.   Are your mother and father living in the United States?   _____

 **Why Is John Crying?**

Topic: feelings

Life Skill/Competency: inquiring about family

Structure: present continuous

Vocabulary
cry—sad	yawn—tired	scratch (her) head—confused
argue—angry	bite (her) nails—worried	bark—scared

Teaching Suggestions

Activity 1

Refer to the procedure on page v.

Ask questions like the following to present the pictures.

What's this person doing?

Why is he/she _____ (cry)ing ?

How is he/she feeling?

Do you ever _____ (cry) ?

Why do people _____ (cry) ?

When do you feel _____ (sad) ?

What do *you* do when you feel _____ (sad) ?

The following is a sample presentation of Picture 1 (John crying).

> Today we're going to talk about feelings. Do you know "feelings"? For example, how am I feeling now [making a happy face]?...Yes, I'm feeling happy. And how am I feeling now [making a sad face]?...Yes, I'm feeling sad. What are some other feelings?...Yes, tired [acting tired], and...cold [acting cold]. These are feelings. Well, now, what do we have here? Is this a pencil or a photo?...Yes, it's a photo. Do any of you have photos with you? Do you have a photo of your chldren, anyone?... Oh, nice, José! What a nice photo of your little girl. Now, let's look at this photo here. Who is this?...It's our old friend, John. But look! What's he doing? Is he smiling?...No, he's not smiling. He's...Yes, he's crying. Poor John! Now, who else cries? I mean, who cries a lot?...Yes, babies cry a lot. And when do babies cry?...Babies cry when they're...Yes. Babies cry when they're hungry. And when do we cry, when we're happy or we're sad? Yes, when we're sad. And when are we sad?... Yes, we're sad when we lose a job. When else are we sad?...Yes, we're sad when our friend goes away. So what's John doing?...Yes, he's crying. And why is he crying?...Yes, because he's sad.

Activity 2

Refer to the procedure on page vi.

Point out that items 4 and 5—*bite her nails* and *scratch her head*—require possessive adjectives. Do a quick review of *his* and *her* by asking three male students and three female students to go to the chalkboard. Ask each of them to write various personal information—first name, last name, address, phone number, social security number, birthdate—on the board. Then ask the class what each student is doing. For example:

T: Ali, please write your phone number....Class, what's Ali doing?

Ss: He's writing *his* phone number.

T: Ana, please write your last name....Class, what's Ana doing?

Ss: She's writing *her* last name.

Grammar Box (page 46 of Student Book)

Refer to the procedure on page viii.

Give students some oral practice making *Why* questions. Bring in pictures of people wearing the following: a heavy coat, a fancy dress, a hard hat, a T-shirt, gloves, and a bathing suit (you'll have to teach this last item). Begin by holding up the pictures one by one and modeling *Why* questions and answers. For example:

> T: (pointing to a man wearing a heavy coat) Why is he wearing a coat?
> Because it's cold outside.

These answers can be used in response to subsequent questions.

> Fancy dress: Because she's going to a party.
> Hard hat: Because he's working.
> T-shirt: Because it's hot outside.
> Gloves: Because it's cold outside.
> Bathing suit: Because she's swimming.

Go through the pictures a second time, asking the questions and having students give the answers. Then go through them a third time, having students make both the questions and the answers.

Activity 3

Refer to the procedure on page ix.

As students look at the picture to the right of the conversation, ask these questions.

> *How many people are in this picture?; What are they doing?*

After you practice the conversations with the students, write the first one on the chalkboard and use it to work on stress and rhythm. Model the dialogue line by line, asking students which syllables in each sentence receive stress. Mark the stressed syllables with dots, as follows.

> Who's crying?
> John is.
> Why is he crying?
> Because he's sad.

Explain that stressed syllables are said louder and held longer than unstressed syllables. Unstressed syllables are said softly and quickly. Practice the two conversations again, helping students produce sentences with the correct stress and rhythm. Then erase the dialogue from the board. Encourage and help students attend to stress and rhythm when they do the pairwork.

Activity 4

Refer to the procedure on page ix.

As students look at the picture to the right of the conversation, ask these questions.

> *Is this a picture of a man or a woman?; What's she doing?; Why?*

Activity 6

After students have practiced these conversations with their partners, ask them to say how you're feeling as you act out the six feelings introduced in this unit. (In addition, pantomime the feeling *fine* by smiling at the class.) As you go through the pantomime, write the seven feelings on the chalkboard. Then, engage students in impromptu dialogues adapting the two models on page 48 of the Student Book. For example:

> T: Menh, do you have a son?
>
> M: Yes.
>
> T: How is he?
>
> M: Not so good.
>
> T: Oh? What's wrong?
>
> M: He's worried about his job.
>
> T: Worried? That's too bad.

Students' responses to the open-ended question *What's wrong?* may not be completely grammatical. However, you should encourage and help them express these feelings and problems in whatever way they can.

Activity 7

After students finish the writing task, have them share some of their sentences with the class.

For further reinforcement of feelings, refer to Expansion Activities 1 and 2.

Expansion Activities

1. To review feelings, list them on the chalkboard. Then read the following pairs of sentences aloud and have students say how the person is feeling. After students identify the feeling for each item, ask them when or in what situations they experience this feeling themselves.

   Mei Li is in the United States. Her husband is living in China. (sad)

   Maria is running. A man is running after her. (scared)

   Tim is studying. He can't understand his homework. (confused)

   Mr. and Mrs. Morgan are talking in loud voices. They're arguing. (angry)

   Lee can't find a job. He has no money. (worried)

   Stan is getting undressed. He's yawning. (tired)

2. Hand each student a flashcard (which you have made before class) with one of the feelings written on it. One by one, have them go to the front of the classroom and act out the feelings. Encourage individual students to ask questions until someone guesses the correct feeling. Then have that person ask *Why?* For example:

   Saelee: Are you worried?

   Roberto: No, I'm not.

   Tran: Are you confused?

   Roberto: Yes, I am.

   Tran: Why?

   Roberto: Because I can't understand the teacher!

Look at the pictures. Complete the conversations.

1.

A: *Is John crying?*

B: Yes, he is.

A: Why is he crying?

B: *Because he's sad.*

2.

A: _____

B: Yes, she is.

A: Why is she biting her nails?

B: _____

3.

A: _____

B: Yes, he is.

A: _____

B: Because he's tired.

4.

A: _____

B: Yes, they are.

A: Why are they arguing?

B: _____

5.

A: _____

B: Yes, he is.

A: _____

B: Because he's scared.

6.

A: _____

B: Yes, she is.

A: Why is she scratching her head?

B: _____

UNIT 8 | What's Maria Doing Tomorrow?

Topic: common activities

Life Skill/Competency: telephone skills

Structure: present continuous

Vocabulary
playing baseball   studying   not doing anything
doing his laundry/laundromat   fixing his car/garage   fishing

Teaching Suggestions
Activity 1

Refer to the procedure on page v.

This unit is atypical. Students will be producing statements just after you have presented the vocabulary, as in the sample presentation. Allow several students to produce each statement, and allow extra time. Ask the following questions to present each picture.

1. Maria's day

   a. What's Maria doing?   (playing baseball)

   b. Where's she playing baseball?   (in the park)

   c. Who's she playing baseball with?   (her mother)

   d. When's she playing baseball?   (in the morning)

   e. How's she getting to the park?   (by bus)

2. Stan's day

   a. What's Stan doing?   (doing his laundry)

   b. Where's he doing his laundry?   (at the laundromat)

   c. How's he getting there?   (by car/He's driving.)

3. John's day

   a. What's John doing?   (fixing his car)

   b. Who's he fixing his car with?   (his father)

   c. Where's he fixing his car?   (in the garage)

   d. When's he fixing his car?   (in the afternoon)

4. Zabu's day

   a. What's Zabu doing?   (nothing)

5. Tim and Kate's day

   a. What are Tim and Kate doing?   (studying)

   b. Where are they studying?   (at school)

   c. Who are they studying with?   (their classmates/friends)

   d. When are they studying?   (all day)

6. Mr. and Mrs. Morgan's day

   a. What are Mr. and Mrs. Morgan doing?   (going fishing)

   b. Where are they going fishing?   (at the beach)

   c. Who are they going with?   (their dog)

   d. How are they getting to the beach?   (They're walking)

The following is a sample presentation of Picture 1 (Maria's day).

> Let's see what Maria is doing tomorrow. Is she going to work, or playing baseball?...She's playing baseball. Anyone here play baseball?...Oh, Pedro, you play baseball. Good. How about you, Chau?... No?... Oh, they don't play much baseball in your country. I see. Now, where is Maria playing baseball [pointing to the trees]?...Yes, she's playing baseball in the park. And who is she playing with? Her father or her mother [pointing to the mother]?...No question about this one; it's her mother. And when is she playing [pointing to sun going up]?...Yes, in the morning. How did you know it was morning, Kim?... Yes, because the sun is going up. Now, how is Maria getting to the park [pointing to the bus]? Is she walking?... No, she's taking the bus. Now look at the picture and listen. [Slowly, pointing to individual parts of the picture:] Maria's playing baseball in the park with her mother in the morning. She's taking the bus there. Who can say that?...Tran, you want to try? Go ahead.

Grammar Box   (page 51 of Student Book)

Refer to the procedure on page viii.

Review the *Wh-* words *what, where, when, how,* and *who.* Ask students to recall the question words they've studied together and write this list on the chalkboard. Next, draw four stick figures on the board and ask students to give them names. Then help students invent stories about the activities of these characters. Begin by pointing to the word *what* and to one of the characters and asking what he or she is doing today. Suggest an answer. Then point to the word *where* and make an appropriate question and answer. As students grasp the idea that they're to use their imaginations in responding to the questions, begin allowing them to make the answers. The dialogue you create should resemble the following.

> T: What's Betsy doing? Visiting her aunt and uncle.
>
> Where is she visiting her aunt and uncle? In Los Angeles.
>
> When is she visiting them?
>
> Ss: In the evening.
>
> T: How is she getting to L.A.?
>
> Ss: She's driving.
>
> T: Who is she going with?
>
> Ss: Her sister.

Point to the other characters and the question words one by one. Have students invent similar stories for all of the characters, making both the questions and the answers.

Grammar Box   (page 52 of Student Book)

Refer to the procedure on page viii.

Review the intonation patterns for yes/no questions (rising) and short answers (rising/falling) by modeling a few questions and answers and drawing arrows above these sentences on the chalkboard. Then ask students questions about what they're doing tomorrow (e.g., *Juana, are you going to the bank tomorrow?*) and have them respond with short answers. Have them repeat the answers as necessary to achieve the correct stress and intonation. Then give prompts, using verb phrases that students are familiar with (e.g., *visit a friend, watch TV*) and have individual students ask and answer the questions. Help them with stress and intonation.

Activity 4

Refer to the procedure on page ix.

As you practice the questions and answers with the students, point out that *this Saturday* and *this weekend,* like *tomorrow,* are used to talk about actions in the future.

Activity 5

Before students do the writing task, ask five or six students to make sentences about what they're doing after class, tomorrow, this Saturday, and this weekend. After the writing task, have students share some of their sentences with the class.

Activity 6

Use this activity to introduce the concept that *Wh-* questions generally have falling intonation. As you model the questions for the students, ask them to listen for whether your voice goes up or down at the end of each sentence. Write three of the questions on the chalkboard and indicate the intonation pattern with falling arrows, as follows.

What are you doing next weekend? ↘

What movie are you going to? ↘

What day are you going? ↘

Help students produce these and other questions in the conversation with falling intonation. Point out that while yes/no questions generally have rising intonation, *Wh-* questions generally have falling intonation.

Before students start the pairwork, call their attention to the fact that *next weekend* and *next summer* are also used to talk about actions in the future. In addition, list these *Wh-*expressions on the chalkboard: *what, what day, what time, who, where,* and *how.* Model the task students will do in pairs by asking three students questions with this series of *Wh-*expressions, pointing to them one by one. Then have members of the class ask you the same series of questions about your plans for the weekend and for the summer.

After students finish the writing task, have them share some of their sentences with the class.

For reinforcement of *Wh-* questions and the present continuous tense, refer to Expansion Activity 1.

Activity 7

Refer to the procedure on page ix.

As students look at the pictures of the places, review them by pointing and asking students to name them. Then ask these questions about the picture of Maria.

Who's in this picture?; Where is she?; What's she doing?; What's she wearing?

Activity 8

Before students start the pairwork, model the dialogue with two or three students, using real (or plastic) telephones if possible. After students finish the pairwork, have them work with their partners to write their own dialogues using one of the places they learned in Unit 2. Then ask pairs of students to perform their dialogues in front of the class, with telephones if possible.

For reinforcement of telephone skills, refer to Expansion Activity 2.

Expansion Activities

1. To review *Wh-* question formation and the present continuous tense, write on the chalkboard (or dictate) a list of short answers (e.g., *by bus, cleaning the house, at 7:00 in the evening*). Have students write the questions.

2. Strip Story. Using the dialogue in Activity 8 as a model, type out a new dialogue and cut it into strips of paper, with one strip per line of text. Put students into pairs and give each pair all of the strips necessary to create the dialogue. (The strips should not be in order.) Ask students to arrange the strips to create a conversation. Then have them practice the conversation aloud.

A.   Read the answers. Then write the missing words at the beginning of the questions.

1.   _____ are you going next weekend?   To Seattle.

2.   _____ are you doing in Seattle?   Visiting friends.

3.   _____ are you going with?   My wife.

4.   _____ are you getting there?   We're taking the bus.

5.   _____ are you going?   Friday night.

B.   Look at the pictures and complete the questions. Then write answers. Use the answers in the box.

Yes, I am.	No, I'm not.	I'm not sure. Maybe.

1.   Are you _____ _____ _____ home after class?

    _____

2.   Are you _____ _____ _____ this evening?

    _____

3.   Are you _____ _____ _____ tonight?

    _____

4.   Are you _____ _____ _____ this week?

    _____

UNIT 9 Is There a Post Office in Your Neighborhood?

Topics: community resources; household items
Life Skill/Competency: street directions
Structure: *there is/are*
Vocabulary

post office	hills	plants	bookshelves
trees	library	dishwasher	ghost
mailbox	restaurants	pictures	closets
tall buildings	movie theater	basement	mice
day-care center	pay phones	stairs	block
parking meters	TV	garage	turn right/left
health clinic	VCR		

Teaching Suggestions
Activity 1

Refer to the procedure on page v.

Ask questions like the following to present the pictures.

> What is this (place)?
>
> What do we do at a _(post office)_?
>
> Do you ever go to a _(post office)_?
>
> Is/Are there _(a post office)_ near your house?
>
> How far is it from your house?
>
> Are there many _post offices_ in your city?

The following is a sample presentation of Picture 1 (post office).

> Today we're going to talk about some more places in town. Let's take a look at this place. What is this? Does anybody know?...Well, what is this [pointing to the stamp]?...Yes, it's a stamp. So what is this place?... Yes, it's a post office. Now what do we do at the post office? Do we go dancing?...No. What do we do?... Yes, we buy stamps. Like this stamp [pointing]. What else do we do at the post office?...Yes, we send letters. What else?...Yes, we send packages at the post office. Now, is there a post office near school?... Yes, there's a post office on Maple Street. How far is it to walk to that post office?...Yes, it's about a five-minute walk to the post office on Maple Street.

Grammar Box   (page 56 of Student Book)

Refer to the procedure on page viii.

Review the intonation pattern for yes/no questions and short answers as you ask students about things in the classroom and places at school. Write two of these questions and answers on the chalkboard. Establish the intonation patterns by modeling the sentences and asking students whether your voice goes up or down. Draw arrows above the sentences indicating that these questions and answers follow the regular pattern for yes/no questions and short answers. For example:

T: Is there a telephone in the classroom?

Ss: No, there isn't.

T: Are there any restrooms at school?

Ss: Yes, there are.

Throughout the practice, help students produce answers with rising/falling intonation.

Activity 4

Refer to the procedure on page v.

Ask questions like the following to present the pictures.

What is this?

Is this a ____(TV)____ or a ____(VCR)____?

Is/Are there ____(a TV)____ in your house?

Is/Are there ____(a TV)____ in our school?

Where do you put/find ____(a TV)____?

What do we use ____(a TV)____ for?

The following is a sample presentation of Pictures 1 and 2 (TV and VCR).

> Today we're going to talk about things in your house. What's this?...Yes, it's a television. Or, we can say...? Yes, "TV" is the same as "television." I think everyone knows what a TV is. But what's this next thing?...Yes, we use it to watch videos, and what do we call it?...Well, is it a clock, or a VCR?...Yes, it's a VCR. And we use a VCR together with what?...Yes, we use a VCR with our TV. And what do we watch on a VCR?...Yes, we watch videos. Videos of what?...Yes, we watch movies on our VCR. And you say you watch your baby on the VCR, Ana? How nice! You make movies of your baby and watch them on the VCR. So, class, is there a VCR in Ana's house?... Yes, there is.

Activity 5

Refer to the procedure on page vi.

Remind students that the singular form of *mice* is *mouse*.

For reinforcement of the vocabulary and questions with *Is/Are there*, refer to Expansion Activities 1 and 2.

Grammar Box   (page 58 of Student Book)

Refer to the procedure on page viii.

Make a list on the chalkboard of singular and plural nouns that might or might not be found in a classroom. Point to the nouns one at a time and have students make sentences about them. For example:

(baby)   There isn't a baby in the classroom.

(chairs)   There are 40 chairs in the classroom.

Activity 6

After students finish the pairwork, have them write six sentences about things in their houses. Later, have them share some of their sentences with the class.

Activity 8

To prepare students for this activity, have a map of the world available for them to view. Before practicing the conversations, have students talk about their hometowns and show where they are on the map. Ask several students these questions.

What country is your hometown in?; What's the name of your hometown?;

Can you please show us where it is on the map?

Before students start the writing task, call their attention to the fact that in the first sentence, they'll need to write their partner's name with an 's. In subsequent sentences, students can continue using possessive nouns or switch to possessive adjectives. After the writing task, have students share some of their sentences with the class.

For reinforcement of vocabulary and sentences with *There is/are*, refer to Expansion Activity 3.

Activity 11

Information Gap. Refer to the procedure on page xi.

Activity 12

After students have finished writing directions, ask the A's for directions to the pay phone, the day-care center, the park, and the hospital, and ask the B's for directions to the library, the movie theater, the laundromat, and the bus stop. Write the directions on the chalkboard.

Expansion Activities

1. Dictate the household vocabulary items on page 58 of the Student Book and have students draw pictures of the items and label them.

2. Review yes/no questions beginning with *Is there* and *Are there* by questioning a few students about things in their houses. Then have students make charts in which they write six household items down the left side and the names of three classmates along the top, similar to the chart below.

	Menh	Lourdes	Van
VCR			
closets			
plants			
basement			
garage			
mice			

Have students interview three of their classmates, asking them yes/no questions and filling in the chart with *yes* and *no*. Remind students to use the correct intonation patterns.

3. Have students draw simple maps of their neighborhoods. Ask them to label the streets, places, and things with vocabulary from pages 18 and 56 of the Student Book. (Remind them that they can use the word *laundromat* too.) Then put this prompted dialogue on the chalkboard.

A: There's a _____ in my neighborhood.

B: Where is it?

A: Next to _____ .

On _____ Street.

On the corner.

Have students talk about their neighborhoods in pairs, using the cues above.

Since students may not be able to draw their neighborhoods from memory, this activity may be more appropriate as a homework assignment for use in class the following day.

A. **Look at the pictures. Write sentences about your neighborhood.**

Example: *There isn't a movie theater in my neighborhood.*

1. _____

2. _____

3. _____

4. _____

B. **Read the questions and write answers about your house. Use the answers in the box.**

Yes, there is.	No, there isn't.	Yes, there are.	No, there aren't.

1. Is there a dishwasher in your house? _____

2. Are there plants in your house? _____

3. Is there a basement in your house? _____

4. Are there bookshelves in your house? _____

5. Is there a VCR in your house? _____

UNIT 10 Where's the Bedroom?

Topic: rooms and furnishings

Life Skill/Competency: rental inquiries

Structure: *there is/are*

Vocabulary

bedroom	bed	sink	stove	washer
hallway	dresser	mirror	oven	dryer
bathroom	closet	bathtub	refrigerator	basement
living room	window	sofa/couch	counter	rug
kitchen	toilet	armchair	microwave	medicine cabinet
yard	scale	lamp	faucet	curtains
garage	shower	stairs	cupboard/cabinet	table

Teaching Suggestions
Activity 1

Refer to the procedure on page v.

Introduce the names of the (lettered) rooms and areas first, and then proceed to the (numbered) furnishings.

Ask questions like the following to present the rooms and areas.

> What room is this?
>
> Is it upstairs or downstairs?
>
> What do we do in a ___(kitchen)___?
>
> Do you have a ___(basement)___ in your house?
>
> What color is the ___(kitchen)___ in your house?
>
> Is the ___(bedroom)___ in your house upstairs or downstairs?

The following is a sample presentation of the *bedroom*.

> What do we have here?...Yes, this is a house. Today we're going to talk about houses. And how many rooms are there in this house?...Yes, there are five rooms [pointing to them]. How many rooms are there in your house, Ali?...Three rooms? What about your house, Chris?...Two rooms? Now then, in this picture, which room is the bedroom?...Yes, room A is the bedroom. What do we do in a bedroom? Do we eat?...No, we sleep in a bedroom. What color is your bedroom, Yukiko?...Your bedroom is white? My bedroom is white, too. Is this bedroom downstairs or upstairs?...Yes, it's upstairs. Well, then, where is the hallway?...Yes, it's B.

Review rooms and areas by asking what letter each one is.

Look at page 64 of the Student Book and ask the following questions to present the furnishings.

> What is this?
>
> Is this a ___(bed)___ or a ___(dresser)___?
>
> Where do we find a ___(dresser)___?
>
> What do we use a ___(dresser)___ for?
>
> Do you have a ___(dresser)___ in your house?
>
> Where is the ___(dresser)___ in your house?
>
> What color is the ___(dresser)___ in your house?

The following is a sample presentation of the *dresser*.

> Let's go back to the bedroom now and look inside. What's this?...Is it a bed or a dresser?...Yes, it's a dresser. Now what do we keep in a dresser?...Do we keep hamburgers?...No, we keep clothes in a dresser. Where is the dresser in this bedroom?...Yes, the dresser is next to the closet. Do you have a dresser in your bedroom, Bao Zhu?...You do? What about you, Amy?...You have a dresser too? What color is your dresser?...Your dresser is brown. And how big is your dresser?

Review furnishings by asking what number each one is.

Activity 2

Refer to the procedure on page vi.

After students finish the pairwork, give them additional practice with the new vocabulary by having them look at page 63 of the Student Book and answer a series of yes/no questions about the house. If the answer is *no*, students should volunteer the correct location. For example:

> T: Are there curtains in the living room?
>
> Ss: Yes, there are.
>
> T: Is there a bedroom downstairs?
>
> Ss: No, there isn't. The bedroom is upstairs.

Activity 3

Before listening to the conversations, review the names of the clothing items pictured above the rooms.

Activity 5

Before listening to the conversation, prepare the class for the activities on this page by asking several students these questions.

> *Are you living in a house or an apartment?; How many bedrooms?;*
>
> *Is your apartment furnished or unfurnished?; What street is it on?;*
>
> *Is there a manager in your building?; Is it a man or a woman?; What's his/her name?*

As students are listening to the conversation, write it on the chalkboard. Then model it line by line. Ask students which syllable is the loudest in each phrase or sentence and mark the primary stress with a dot. Then have students tell you whether your voice rises or falls at the end of each utterance. Indicate rising intonation with an arrow going up and falling intonation with an arrow going down.

Call students' attention to the different intonation patterns in the conversation. Remind them that while yes/no questions generally have rising intonation, *Wh-* questions and statements generally have falling intonation. As students practice the conversation with their partners, circulate to help with stress and intonation.

Activity 6

For reinforcement of language related to housing inquiries, refer to Expansion Activity 3.

Activity 7

Information Gap. Refer to the procedure on page xi.

After students have finished the Information Gap activity, ask the A's for the location of Zabu, the lamp, the rug, and the curtains, and ask the B's for the location of the cupboard, the pictures, the mirror, and the mice. Write the locations on the chalkboard.

For reinforcement of vocabulary for rooms and furniture, refer to Expansion Activities 1 and 2.

Expansion Activities

1. Give students lots of additional practice on the vocabulary in this unit. First, bring in several pictures of different pieces of furniture. Show them to the class one by one, naming the piece of furniture correctly or incorrectly. Have students respond with *yes* or *no*. Then go through the pictures again and have students name them.

   Next, draw six columns on the chalkboard and label them *bedroom, hallway, bathroom, living room, kitchen,* and *basement*. Show the students flashcards (which you have made before class) with the names of furniture, appliances, and fixtures, and have students read the words. Go through the flashcards again. Make true/false statements about which room each object belongs in, and have students respond with *yes* or *no*. For example:

   T: (holding up *sink*) It belongs in the living room.

   Ss: No.

   T: It belongs in the bathroom.

   Ss: Yes.

   Tape each item to the chalkboard in the correct column.

2. Have students draw a diagram of one or two rooms in their homes. Show them how to do this by drawing an example from your home on the chalkboard and labeling the furniture, fixtures, and appliances.

   After students finish their diagrams, write a dialogue on the chalkboard. For example:

   A: There's an armchair in my living room.

   B: Where is it?

   A: It's next to the sofa.

   Using this dialogue as a model, talk with students about several of the furnishings in the room you drew. Then erase the dialogue and have students talk with their partners about the rooms they drew.

3. Strip Story. Using the dialogue in Activity 5 as a model, type out a new dialogue and cut it into strips of paper, with one strip per line of text. Put students into pairs and give each pair all of the strips necessary to create the dialogue. (The strips should not be in order.) Have them work together to put the strips in the correct order. Then have them practice the conversation aloud.

A. Look at the picture on page 63. Write the missing words.

1. The curtains are in the ___living room___ ___on___ the window.

2. The mirror is in the _____ _____ the sink.

3. The stairs are in the _____ _____ the sofa.

4. The rug is in the _____ _____ the dresser.

5. The microwave is in the _____ _____ the counter.

6. The lamp is in the _____ _____ the corner.

7. The scale is in the _____ _____ the bathtub.

8. The washer is in the _____ _____ the dryer.

B. Write sentences about your house or apartment.

Examples: Is there a telephone in your house?

**Yes, there is. It's in the kitchen on the counter.**

Are there stairs in your house?

**No, there aren't.**

1. Is there an armchair in your house?

   _____

2. Is there a rug in your house?

   _____

3. Are there cupboards in your house?

   _____

4. Are there curtains in your house?

   _____

5. Is there a medicine cabinet in your house?

   _____

6. Is there a washer in your house?

   _____

What Time Is It, Please?

Topic: daily routine

Life Skills/Competencies: telling time; relating personal problems

Structure: present tense

Vocabulary
get up	eat lunch	brush your teeth
take a shower	get home/return home	go to bed/go to sleep
shave	eat dinner	noon
eat breakfast	watch TV	midnight
leave home	do homework	

Teaching Suggestions

Activity 3

After students finish the listening activity, check their comprehension of the times and work with the class on sentence rhythm. Write each sentence on the chalkboard with dots above the stressed syllables. For example:

It's nine forty-five.

It's eight thirty.

It's four fifteen.

It's a quarter after three.

Model each sentence for the students. Then clap the rhythm, clapping hard on the stressed syllables and softly and quickly on the unstressed syllables. Have the students first clap the rhythm and then repeat the sentence. Go through the sentences again, saying them quickly and clapping only on the stressed syllables. Have students repeat.

Activity 4

Refer to the procedure on page v.

As you ask students when *they* do the various activities, if a student attempts a negative response, demonstrate the answer *I don't _____*, clarifying the meaning if necessary. For faster classes, suggest answers utilizing the time reference words from page 73 of the Student Book (i.e., *at, about, before,* and *after*) before the formal presentation of these time expressions.

Ask questions like the following to present the pictures.

What is he/she doing in this picture?

When do people __(get up)__?

Do *you* __(watch TV)__ every day?

What time do *you* __(get up)__?

Where do people __(do homework)__?

Where do *you* __(do homework)__?

The following is a sample presentation of Picture 1 (When do you get up?).

Today we're going to talk about what time we do things every day. Let's look at this picture. Is this person getting up, or going to sleep [pointing to the sun]?... Yes; he's getting up. Now, when do we get up? Do we get up in the morning or at night?...Yes, we get up in the morning. And where do we get up? In the kitchen?... No! We get up in the bedroom. Now, Jacques, when do you get up every day?...At 5:00?! My goodness! And what about you, Gunther? When do you get up every morning?...At 8:30? Now that's more like it!

Grammar Box   (page 73 of Student Book)

Refer to the procedure on page viii.

Write these cues for a dialogue on the chalkboard.

<u>Right now</u>

A: What are you doing now?

B: _____.

A: What are you _____ing?

B: _____.

<u>Usually/Every day</u>

A: What do you usually _____ for _____?

B: _____.

Draw a clock reading 7:00 and a rising sun. Then point to the clock face and pantomime eating breakfast. Have the students ask you questions, following the cues on the board. For example:

Ss: What are you doing now?

T: Eating breakfast.

Ss: What are you eating?

T: Bread with jam.

Ss: What do you usually eat for breakfast?

T: Cereal.

Pantomime drinking something and have students ask the same sequence of questions. Then change the clock to read 12:00 (for lunch) and 6:00 (for dinner) and go through the dialogue four more times, twice using the verb *eat* and twice using *drink*.

To give students practice making *When* questions in the present tense, write these cues for a dialogue on the chalkboard.

A: Are you _____ing tonight?

B: _____.

A: When do you usually _____?

B: _____.

Pantomime the actions *take the bus, cook a meal, play baseball, watch TV,* and *take a shower* and have students ask you questions following the cues.

Activity 7

As you practice the conversations with the students, call their attention to the many short responses, beginning with different prepositions, that are appropriate. After the pairwork, ask several students questions to reinforce the time expressions they've learned.

For further reinforcement, refer to Expansion Activities 1 and 2.

Activity 8

To further review the feelings, pantomime and have students identify them.

Activity 9

After students do the pairwork, have them continue working with their partners to write an original conversation based on the models. When they've finished, have several pairs of students share their dialogues with the class.

Expansion Activities

1. Give a dictation to reinforce recognition of time expressions. First, have students number their papers from one to ten. Then make ten statements. For example: *I leave home at 8:15.* Tell students to write whatever time expressions they hear.

2. Have students make charts in which they write their daily schedules. Show them how to do this by writing the beginning of your daily schedule in a chart on the chalkboard, similar to the chart below.

7:00	get up eat breakfast
7:30	take a shower get dressed
8:00	leave home take the bus
8:30	go to work

Put these cues on the chalkboard.

A: What do you usually do at _____?

B: _____.

Ask several students what they do at various times during the day and have them respond with short answers. Then have them ask you questions about your daily schedule. Finally, erase the cues and have pairs of students ask and answer questions about their schedules.

A. Look at the pictures. Write questions and answers.

Example: <u>*When do you eat lunch?*</u>   <u>*At 1:00.*</u>

1. _____   _____

2. _____   _____

3. _____   _____

4. _____   _____

B. Match the sentences.

1. Mr. and Mrs. Morgan are yawning.   She's sad.

2. Tim is scratching his head.   They're tired.

3. May is crying.   They're angry.

4. Kate is biting her nails.   He's confused.

5. Zabu is barking.   She's worried.

6. Maria and Stan are arguing.   He's scared.

UNIT 12 | Do You Work on Sundays?

Topic: habitual activities

Life Skill/Competency: talking about work

Structure: present tense

Vocabulary

work on Sundays	tell the truth	full-time job
drink tea	eat a lot of fish	part-time job
take the bus to school	sing in the shower	lunch break
stay home on weekends	get up early	hours
go to bed late	play tennis	boss
go home after class	go to church	

Teaching Suggestions

Activity 1

Refer to the procedure on page v.

Before beginning this presentation, write *Do you...?* on the chalkboard, reminding the students that *Do* questions refer to *usually, every day*, or *sometimes*. Then tell the class that the two answers to this question are *Yes, I do* and *No, I don't*.

Ask questions like the following to present the pictures.

> Do you _(drink tea)_?
>
> Do you *like* ____(work)___ *ing*?
>
> Do you _(play tennis)_ every day/week?
>
> Do you *always* _(tell the truth)_?
>
> Does your wife/husband _(drink tea)_?
>
> Why do/don't you _(get up early)_?
>
> When/Where do you _(play tennis)_?

The following is a sample presentation of Picture 1 (Do you work on Sundays?).

> Today we're going to talk about things that we do, and things we don't do. Let's take a look at this picture. What's this person doing? Is he eating, or is he working?...Yes, he's working. Now, what are these letters across the top of the picture [pointing]?...Let's see, seven letters, seven days of the week. Any ideas?...Yes, Sunday, Monday, Tuesday...And what day is this [pointing to the circled "S"]?...Yes, it's Sunday. Now tell me, Victor, do you work on Sundays?...No, you don't, huh? What about you, Marja? Do you work on Sundays?...Yes, you do. Every Sunday?...Oh, just sometimes. And do you like working on Sundays?...You don't like it very much. I wouldn't like it either.

Activity 4

Refer to the procedure on page ix.

Review the rising intonation pattern for yes/no questions and the rising/falling pattern for short answers. First, write the two conversations on the chalkboard. Then model them line by line and ask students whether your voice goes up or down at the end of each sentence. Draw arrows above the sentences to indicate the correct intonation patterns. Have students repeat the sentences with the correct intonation. Then erase the conversations. As students do the pairwork, help them with intonation.

After students finish the pairwork, reinforce the new structure and review familiar verb phrases by asking questions like these.

T: Danai, do you watch movies?

D: Yes, I do.

T: When do you watch movies?

D: On the weekends.

Next, hold up flashcards (which you have made before class) with phrases from Units 5, 6, 8, and 11. Choose one student to ask the question and another student to answer it. Verb phrases suitable for this activity include the following.

watch movies	swim	visit friends	run
buy food	dance	clean the house	wash the dishes
write letters	drink coffee	play baseball	do the laundry
go fishing	eat breakfast	watch TV	do homework

Grammar Box (page 77 of Student Book, middle)

Refer to the procedure on page viii.

Ask students if they have various school supplies and apparel—pens, pencils, books, notebooks, paper, watches, hats, gloves, and bags. For example:

T: Do you have a notebook, Phu?

Ph: Yes, I do.

T: Do you have gloves, Li Qing?

LQ: No, I don't.

Activity 5

For reinforcement of questions with *Do you have...?*, refer to the Expansion Activity.

Grammar Box (page 78 of Student Book)

Refer to the procedure on page viii.

Write these cues on the chalkboard.

on Fridays	in the morning
on Saturdays	in the afternoon
on Sundays	in the evening
on Mondays	at night

Point to the cues and have students make affirmative and negative statements about when they work.

Activity 6

As you practice the conversations with the students, explain that *Me too* is a rejoinder used when two people are making the same affirmative statement, and that *Me neither* is used when two people are making the same negative statement. They cannot be used if one person's statement is positive and the other person's statement is negative.

In addition, teach students the stress and intonation pattern of these rejoinders. Model them for the students and ask which word is louder in each phrase. Mark the primary stress with a dot. Then ask whether your voice goes up or down, and indicate the intonation pattern with a falling arrow, as follows.

Me too.↘   Me neither.↘

Have students repeat these phrases as necessary.

Finally, give students additional practice by making statements about yourself to which students must add rejoinders. Help them with stress and intonation as they respond. For example:

I drink coffee.	What about you?
I don't play baseball.	
I don't drive a truck.	
I teach English.	
I cook every day.	
I don't fix my car.	

Activity 7

After students finish the writing task, have them share their sentences with the class.

Activities 8 and 9

Refer to the procedure on page x.

As you present the vocabulary items, ask a few students these questions.

Do you have a job, (Mario)?; How many hours a week do you work?;

Class, is his job full-time or part-time?; When do you eat lunch, (Mario)?;

Class, when is his lunch break?; When do you start work, (Mario)?;

When do you get home?; Class, does he have good hours or bad hours?;

Who's your boss, (Mario)?; Do you have a good boss?;

Class, does he have a good boss?

Activity 11

After students finish the writing task, have them share some of their sentences with the class.

Expansion Activity

Have students do a mingling activity in which they move around the classroom asking questions of several other students. Pass out copies of (or have students copy from the chalkboard) the following form.

Find 3 people with a washer and dryer.	Find 3 people with a VCR.
1. _____	1. _____
2. _____	2. _____
3. _____	3. _____
Find 3 people with a garage.	Find 3 people with a basement.
1. _____	1. _____
2. _____	2. _____
3. _____	3. _____

Before starting the activity, read the instructions with the students and model the task. Circulate and ask several students if they have a washer and dryer. Write the names of those who do on your form. Then have all students stand up and begin interviewing their classmates.

UNIT 12 EXERCISES

A. **Look at the pictures. Write questions with *Do you...?***

Example: 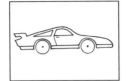 *Do you have a car?*

1.  _____

2.  _____

3.  _____

4. 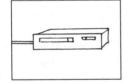 _____

B. **Read the questions and write answers. Use the answers in the box.**

Yes, I am.	No, I'm not.	Yes, I do.	No, I don't.

1. Do you sing in the shower? _____

2. Are you working this Saturday? _____

3. Are you going to the post office this week? _____

4. Do you come to school by bus? _____

5. Do you always tell the truth? _____

6. Are you going shopping tomorrow? _____

UNIT 13　How Do You Get to Work?

Topic:　habitual activities

Life Skill/Competency:　public transportation

Structure:　present tense

Vocabulary　　usually　　　never　　　　get on
　　　　　　　　sometimes　　work clothes　　get off
　　　　　　　　always　　　 casual clothes　fare
　　　　　　　　It depends　　dress up

Teaching Suggestions
Activity 1

Refer to the procedure on page v.

Look at the second page of the unit as you present the pictures on the first page, asking students the target question for each picture. As you ask these questions, help students with their responses, using the answers on page 83 of the Student Book as a guide. Write the boldfaced frequency expressions from page 83 on the chalkboard as you progress through the presentation. Explain the meaning of these expressions and leave them on the board for students to refer to as they answer your questions.

The following is a sample presentation of Picture 1 (How do you get to work?).

> Today we're going to talk some more about things we do. Shao Lin, how [pointing to the word by the picture] do you get to work?...Well, do you walk? Do you drive? Do you swim?...I see. You walk to work. And what about you, Tamim? How do you get to work?...By car. You drive to work. And you, Sho? How do you get to work?...You take the bus. And what about you, Ursula? How do you get to work?

Activity 3

Ask the questions from Activity 2 and then have students repeat the answers after you.

To illustrate the difference between *work clothes, casual clothes,* and *dress up,* show the class pictures of (1) someone with overalls and a hard hat or someone in a uniform, (2) someone in casual pants and a T-shirt, and (3) someone wearing a suit and tie or a dress and high heels. You may also want to introduce some new clothing vocabulary for the apparel in the pictures.

Grammar Box　(page 84 of Student Book)

Refer to the procedure on page viii.

Ask several students what they do on various days and nights of the week.

Activity 5

Refer to the procedure on page ix.

Prepare students for the activity by asking these questions.

> *What is a neighbor?; Do you have neighbors?; Do you talk to your neighbors?;*
>
> *Do you like your neighbors?; Who's talking in this conversation?*

After listening to the conversation and practicing it with the class, write the two sets of cues at the bottom of page 84 of the Student Book on the chalkboard. Ask three or four students questions similar to the questions in this dialogue, pointing to the *Wh-* words as you use them in your questions. Then point to the time expressions one by one and have the students ask you two questions about each habitual activity you mention.

For reinforcement of frequency expressions, refer to Expansion Activity 1.

Activity 6

As you introduce the vocabulary items, ask several students these questions.

Do you take the bus to work/school?; Where do you get on?;

Where do you get off?; How much is the fare?

Prepare students for the activities on pages 85 and 86 of the Student Book by asking these questions.

If you don't know what bus to take, what do you do?;

Who can you call?; Who's calling in this conversation?

Use this activity to review stress and intonation. As students are listening to the conversation, write it on the chalkboard. Then model it line by line. Ask students which syllable is the loudest in each phrase or sentence and mark the primary stress with a dot. Then have students tell you whether your voice goes up or down at the end of each utterance. Indicate rising intonation with an arrow going up and falling intonation with an arrow going down. Ask the students why the only sentence with rising intonation is *Can I help you?* Help them recall that in general yes/no questions have rising intonation, and *Wh-* questions and statements have falling intonation. As you practice the conversation with the students, help them with stress and intonation.

Activity 9

Before students start the pairwork, model the task by telling the class about a bus you take. For example:

I take the #30 bus.

I get on at Stockton Street.

I get off at Market Street.

The fare is $1.00.

After students finish the writing task, have them share their sentences with the class.

For reinforcement and expansion of language related to transportation, refer to Expansion Activity 2.

Expansion Activities

1. Review the adverbs of frequency introduced in this unit. Write *always, usually, sometimes,* and *never* on the chalkboard and ask students to write two statements about habits with each adverb. After they finish writing, have them share some of their sentences with the class.

2. For a more challenging activity, bring in city maps indicating major bus routes. Put students in groups of three or four and hand each group a map. First, help them locate some city landmarks—important buildings, parks, hospitals, schools, and so on. Then ask these questions.

   I'm at _____. I'm going to _____.

   What bus do I take?

   Where do I get on?

   Where do I get off?

Next, write a list of places to go to and from on the chalkboard. For example:

downtown ➡ Mercy Hospital

school ➡ downtown

federal building ➡ bus station

Manley Park ➡ City Library

Have the groups of students gather information about bus numbers and where to get on and off. Then ask the class the same series of questions about each destination.

Complete the conversations. Use these words and phrases: *How, How long, How many, What kind, What time, When, Where, Who,* **and** *Who...with.*

1. A: _____ do you play tennis?

    B: At Morton Park.

    A: _____ do you play _____?

    B: My girlfriend.

2. A: _____ do you call on the weekends?

    B: My mother.

    A: _____ _____ do you talk?

    B: Half an hour.

3. A: _____ do you go to church?

    B: At 10:00 on Sunday morning.

    A: _____ _____ of clothes do you wear?

    B: I dress up.

4. A: _____ _____ do you go to bed?

    B: At midnight.

    A: _____ _____ do you usually sleep?

    B: Seven hours.

5. A: _____ do you go swimming?

    B: At China Beach.

    A: _____ do you get there?

    B: I drive.

6. A: _____ do you work?

    B: At a shoe factory.

    A: _____ _____ days do you work every week?

    B: Five days a week.

Where Do You Keep Your Money?

UNIT 14

Topic: stores and merchandise

Life Skills/Competencies: banking; inquiring about store hours

Structure: present tense

Vocabulary
bank—keep your money
drug store—buy medicine
barber shop/hair salon—get a haircut
supermarket/grocery store—buy food
department store—buy clothes
second-hand store/thrift shop—
buy used things

hardware store—buy tools
auto repair shop—fix your car
furniture store—buy chairs, beds,
and other furniture
gas station—get gas
produce store—buy fruit and vegetables
parking lot—park your car

Teaching Suggestions
Activity 1

Refer to the procedure on page v.

When you ask what people do at the different stores, students' responses (during the presentation and during conversation practice) needn't be restricted to those listed on page 88 of the Student Book. The captions in the book are for students' reference but can be varied or expanded upon.

Ask questions like the following to present the pictures.

What (place) is this?

What do we do/buy at a ___(bank)___?

What's the name of *your* ___(bank)___?

How far is your ___(bank)___ from your house?

Is there a ___(bank)___ near your house?

Is there a ___(bank)___ near school?

The following is a sample presentation of Picture 1 (the bank).

> Today we're going to talk about stores and other places in town. First let's look at this place. What's this, do you think? It's a place with lots of money!...Yes. It's a bank. Now, what do you do at a bank? Do you keep your children at the bank?... No. Do you keep your car at the bank?...No again. Well, what do you keep at the bank?...Yes, you keep your money at the bank. Aziz, do you keep your money at the bank, or under your bed?...You keep it at the bank. And what bank do you keep your money at?...At First Bank. How far is First Bank from your house? Five minutes? Ten minutes?...I see. About a five-minutes' walk.

Activity 2

After students finish the pairwork, show them flashcards (which you have made before class) with the names of the stores. Hold them up one by one and have students read the words. Then go through the flashcards again. As you hold each one up, say any one of the verb phrases introduced on page 88 of the Student Book. If the activity you mention can be done at the store written on the flashcard, students should say *yes*. If not, students should say *no* and offer information about what can be done in that store. For example:

T: (holding up a flashcard that says *second-hand store*) You buy used things here.

Ss: Yes.

T: (holding up a flashcard that says *barber shop*) You fix your car here.

Ss: No.

T: Then what do you do here?

Ss: You get a haircut.

For further reinforcement, refer to Expansion Activity 1.

Activity 3

To reinforce the phrases in the grammar note, write them on the chalkboard and ask students about the location of stores or public buildings near your school. Ask these questions.

Is there a _____ near school?; How far is it?

Before students start working in pairs, ask three or four students about stores near their homes following the models on page 89 of the Student Book.

Activities 4 and 5

Refer to the procedure on page ix.

To prepare the class for the activities on this page, ask several students these questions.

Do you have a bank account?; What's the name of your bank?; Where is it?

For reinforcement of language related to banking, refer to Expansion Activities 2 and 3.

Activity 7

After students finish the listening activity, check their comprehension of the times and review stress and rhythm, as follows.

First, write the sentences on the chalkboard. Say each sentence aloud. Have the students tell you which syllables are stressed and which are unstressed. Mark the stressed syllables with a dot. For example:

It's eight ten.　　It's twelve fifty-five.　　It's twenty past nine.

Next, point to the sentences one by one and have students first clap the rhythm and then say the sentence aloud. Go through the sentences a third time, saying them quickly and clapping only on the stressed syllables. Have students repeat after you.

Activity 8

Refer to the procedure on page x.

Prepare students for the listening activity by asking these questions.

If you don't know what time a store opens, what do you do?;

Can you call on the telephone?; Where do you get the phone number?

For more practice asking for opening and closing times, refer to Expansion Activity 4.

Expansion Activities

1. To review the names of the stores, read each of the following short conversations aloud and have students say in which store they would be likely to hear such a conversation. To indicate when the speaker changes, use dolls or puppets, or draw two stick figures on the chalkboard and point to them as you speak.

   A: What size are these shoes?

   B: They're size 8.

   A: Excuse me. Where's the coffee?

   B: The coffee? It's on aisle 5.

A: Can you please cash this check?

B: Do you have an account with us?

A: Yes, I do.

A: Excuse me. Where can I get this medicine?

B: The pharmacy is at the back of the store.

A: Do you want a shave and a haircut?

B: Just a haircut, please.

A: Can I park my car here?

B: Yes. There's a place in the corner.

A: Thank you.

A: How much is this chair?

B: It's $89.00. That chair over there is only $45.00.

A: What year is your car?

B: 1989.

A: What's wrong with it?

B: It won't start.

A: This sweater is only 95¢!

B: Wow! That's really cheap!

A: Are these tomatoes on sale?

B: Yes, they are. They're only 49¢ a pound.

2. Strip Story. Using the dialogue on page 90 of the Student Book as a model, type out a new dialogue and cut it into strips of paper, with one strip per line of text. Put students into pairs of three and give each pair all of the strips necessary to create the dialogue. (The strips should not be in order.) Have them work together to put the strips in the correct order. Then have them practice the conversation aloud.

3. To give students practice writing checks, photocopy three blank checks. Give copies to the students. First, have them print their names, phone numbers, and addresses in the top left corner of each check. Then dictate instructions and have students write and sign the three checks. For example: *It's October 25, 1996. You're buying a pair of pants at Lane's Department Store. The pants are expensive—they're $36.78. Write a check to Lane's Department Store for $36.78. When you're finished, sign your name.*

4. Ask students to visit four stores in their neighborhoods and gather information about the opening and closing times on weekdays, Saturdays, and Sundays. Write these two questions on the chalkboard and have students practice asking them.

What time do you open on weekdays?/Saturdays?/Sundays?

What time do you close on weekdays?/Saturdays?/Sundays?

Have students write down the names and the opening and closing times of the stores they find out about and hand the information in to you as homework.

A. Match the stores with what you do in them.

1. department store   You buy tools here.

2. auto repair shop   You get your hair cut here.

3. drug store   You buy clothes here.

4. hardware store   They fix your car here.

5. secondhand store   You buy fruit and vegetables here.

6. gas station   You buy used things here.

7. hair salon   You buy medicine here.

8. produce store   You get gas here.

B. Write the answers.

Example: Where do you keep your money?   *At Bayview Federal Bank.*

How far is it from your house?   *Five blocks.*

1. Where do you buy milk?   _____

How far is it from your house?   _____

2. Where do you buy clothes?   _____

How far is it from your house?   _____

3. Where do you get a haircut?   _____

How far is it from your house?   _____

4. Where do you keep your money?   _____

How far is it from your house?   _____

5. Where do you buy fruit and vegetables?   _____

How far is it from your house?   _____

6. Where do you get gas?   _____

How far is it from your house?   _____

7. Where do you buy medicine?   _____

How far is it from your house?   _____

 **UNIT 15** # Where's the Supermarket?

Topic: street locations

Life Skill/Competency: grocery shopping

Structure: *there is/are*

Vocabulary

on First Street		on the corner of Third and Main	
between Park Street and Lake Avenue		across from the hospital	
in the middle of the block		next to the drug store	
pound	each	orange juice	eggs
dozen	lemons	cookies	onions
quart	potatoes	melons	apples

Teaching Suggestions

Activity 1

Refer to the procedure on page v.

For each picture, ask *Where's the ____(supermarket)____?* Then elicit familiar examples of the street location being taught, as in the sample presentation below.

> Today we're going to talk more about locations. We're going to talk about where things are on the street. Look at this picture. Remember what kind of store this is [pointing]?...Yes, it's a supermarket. Now where is the supermarket? Is it on Green Street?...No. Yes, it's on First Street. And what about our school? Where is our school?...Yes, it's on Filbert Street. Now, what about your house, Yuk? Where's your house?...I see, it's on Stockton Street. And your house, Luis?

Activity 2

Refer to the procedure on page vi.

Before students start the pairwork, give them more practice with map reading and the new prepositions. On the chalkboard, draw a simple map that includes your school, a few of the surrounding streets, and a few buildings. Label the school, streets, and buildings, soliciting students' input as you go along. Then ask a series of questions. For example:

> *Is our school on Green Street? No? What street is it on?;*
>
> *Is it between Seventh and Pine?; Is it in the middle of the block or on the corner?;*
>
> *Is it across from the supermarket? No? What's it across from?;*
>
> *Is it next door to the library?*

Activity 4

Refer to the procedure on page ix.

As students look at the picture, ask these questions.

> *How many people are in this picture?;*
>
> *Who are they? (a tourist and a businessman); What is the tourist doing?;*
>
> *How does the businessman look? Is he happy? Why not? (free speculation)*

As you practice the conversation with the students, call their attention to the rising intonation pattern of the yes/no questions and the falling intonation pattern of the statements. Have them repeat the sentences with the correct intonation.

In addition, teach the pronunciation of *have to* in informal speech. Write the sentence *I have to go now!* on the chalkboard. Cross out the words *have to* and above them write *hafta*. Explain that this is often the pronunciation *have to* in spoken English. Have students repeat the sentence *I hafta go now!* until they pronounce it correctly. Then say these verb phrases one by one: *work, run, clean the house, wash the dishes, get dressed, do the laundry, eat lunch,* and *do my homework.* Have students produce sentences like the following.

> I *hafta* work now.

> I *hafta* run now.

Encourage and help students to use the phrase *I have to go now!* as they do the pairwork.

For reinforcement of street locations, refer to Expansion Activity 1.

Activities 5 and 6

Information Gap. Refer to the procedure on page xi.

Before starting the activities, review the foods and containers introduced in Unit 2 on pages 21 and 22 of the Student Book. Hold up food items or pictures and have students name them. As each item is named, ask several students if they eat the food and, if so, for which meal.

> T: Beatriz, do you eat cereal?
>
> B: Yes, I do.
>
> T: For dinner?
>
> B: No. For breakfast.

To illustrate the word *pound*, hold up a plastic bag containing a pound of beans or tomatoes or some other familiar food. Pass this bag around the classroom so students can feel how heavy it is. Illustrate the word *quart* with a quart-sized carton of milk.

After introducing the new food items, check students' comprehension. Put food, realia, or large pictures of the foods in different places around the classroom. Ask students to point to the items as you say them. Then hold up the items or pictures and ask students to name them.

Activity 7

After students have finished the writing task, ask the A's for the price of the orange juice, cookies, onions, and apples, and ask the B's for the price of the potatoes, melons, milk, and eggs. Write the information on the chalkboard.

For reinforcement of the foods, refer to Expansion Activities 2 and 3.

Expansion Activities

1. Make and pass out copies of a simple street map that is blank except for street names and two stores, which are labeled. Have students repeat the names of the streets and note the location of the two stores. Then give a series of commands in which you instruct students to draw and label various stores and buildings, such as hospitals, libraries, and health clinics, on their maps. For example:

   Draw a drugstore across from the supermarket.

   Draw an auto repair shop on the corner of Fifth Street and Main Street.

   After students finish their maps, have them work in pairs, asking and answering questions about the location of the stores. Last, have them write complete sentences about the location of six or eight stores.

2. To review the foods introduced in this unit, dictate the names of the foods and have students draw pictures and label them. Then ask students whether they eat or drink these foods (and the foods from Unit 2) in their countries. Finally, have students categorize the foods according to whether they eat or drink them for breakfast, lunch, or dinner.

3. Pass out shopping lists and ask students to visit a local grocery store to gather information about the price and location of the foods introduced in this unit. For homework, have them write two sentences about each food. For example:

Potatoes are 49¢ a pound. They're on aisle 1 in the middle of the aisle.

Orange juice is $1.99 a quart. It's between the milk and the meat.

A. **Look at the map on page 95. Write the missing words.**

1. The hardware store is __*on the corner of*__ Second Street and Park Avenue.

2. The furniture store is _____ the park.

3. The bank is _____ the restaurant and the hair salon.

4. The department store is _____ the post office.

5. The gas station is _____ Third Street _____ River and Park.

   It's _____ the block.

6. The movie theater is _____ First and River.

7. The pay phone is _____ the zoo.

8. The hospital is _____ Lake Avenue _____ Second and Third.

B. **Look at the pictures. Write sentences about your neighborhood.**

Example:

The bank is on Steiner Street across from the post office.

1.

   _____

2.

   _____

3.

   _____

4.

   _____

UNIT 16 | **What Time Does May Leave Home?**

Topic: daily routine

Life Skill/Competency: filling out a schedule

Structure: present tense

Vocabulary

leave home	take a coffee break	relax
catch the bus	eat lunch	cook dinner
get to work	finish work/get off work	read the paper
start work/begin work	get home	watch TV

Teaching Suggestions

Activity 1

Refer to the procedure on page v.

Ask questions like the following to present the pictures.

What's May doing (in this picture)?

Is she _(leaving home)_ or _(catching the bus)_?

When does she _(catch the bus)_ every day?

Do *you* _(catch the bus)_ every day?

What time do *you* usually _(catch the bus)_?

Where do you usually _(catch the bus)_?

The following is a sample presentation of Picture 1 (What time do you leave home?).

> Today we're going to talk about May's daily routine. Let's look at this picture. What's May doing? Is she watching TV, or is she leaving home?...Yes, she's leaving home. By the way, when do we leave home— at night?...No, we leave home in the morning. And what time does May leave home every morning [pointing to the clock]?...Yes, she leaves home at 7:25. What about you, Delma? What time do you leave home every morning?...I see, at half past eight. Not bad. And what about you, Mehmet? What time do you leave home?

Activity 3

Refer to the procedure on page vii.

Before starting the listening task, write *most mornings, most days, most nights,* and *most evenings* on the chalkboard and explain that these expressions are roughly equivalent to *usually.*

Grammar Box (page 101 of Student Book)

Refer to the procedure on page viii.

Ask two male and two female students to go to the front of the classroom. Divide the rest of the class in half. Ask each of the four individuals the two questions from the grammar box and have them give short answers. Then have half of the class ask a third-person question that the other half must answer. For example:

T: Mai, what time do you start work?

M: At 8:00.

Ss1: What time does she start work?

Ss2: At 8:00.

T: Rubens, where do you live?

R: On Eighteenth Street.

Ss1: Where does he live?

Ss2: On Eighteenth Street.

Grammar Box (page 102 of Student Book)

Refer to the procedure on page viii.

Review intonation for yes/no questions and short answers. Write the following sentences on the chalkboard and ask students to recall the intonation for yes/no questions (rising) and for short answers (rising/falling). Draw arrows above the sentences.

Q: Does he have a sister?   A: Yes, he does.

Q: Does she have children?   A: No, she doesn't.

Have students repeat the questions and answers using the correct intonation. Then erase the sentences and do the same type of question-and-answer transformation as above. Ask four students to go to the front of the classroom and divide the rest of the class in half. Review the work-related vocabulary introduced in Unit 12—*full-time job, part-time job, lunch break, hours,* and *boss*—as you ask the students at the front of the classroom about their jobs. For example:

T: Khalid, do you have a full-time job?

K: Yes, I do.

Ss1: Does he have a full-time job?

Ss2: Yes, he does.

T: Do you have good hours?

K: No, I don't.

Ss1: Does he have good hours?

Ss2: No, he doesn't.

Activity 5

Refer to the procedure on page ix.

After students finish the pairwork, have them practice writing yes/no questions in the third person. First, brainstorm activities people do to have fun (e.g., *swim, dance, play baseball*) and list them on the chalkboard. Then ask students to write five questions about members of their partners' families. For example:

Does your brother play baseball?; Does your sister dance?

After students write the questions, have them interview their partners.

Grammar Box (page 103 of Student Book)

Refer to the procedure on page viii.

Use the list of fun activities students generated for Activity 5 to practice the third-person singular. Point to one of the activities and have a student make a statement about him- or herself. For example: *I don't swim.* Have the rest of the class transform the statement into the third-person singular. For example: *She doesn't swim.*

To practice transforming the verb *have,* list work-related vocabulary (i.e., *full-time job, part-time job, lunch break, hours, boss*) on the chalkboard and follow the same procedure as above. Likewise, to practice transforming the verb *go,* brainstorm places to go inside and outside the city (e.g., *the park, the movies, the beach*) and list them on the chalkboard. Follow the same procedure as above, having students make statements about themselves that the other students must transform into the third-person singular.

Activity 8

After students finish the writing task, have them share some of their sentences with the class.

For reinforcement of affirmative and negative statements in the present tense, refer to Expansion Activities 1 and 2.

Expansion Activities

1. To give students additional practice making both affirmative and negative statements in the third-person singular, have them make charts in which they copy six verb phrases down the left side and write the names of three classmates along the top, similar to the chart below.

	Suhua	Thuy	Carlos
like American movies			
like hot dogs			
have a red car			
have a driver's license			
go fishing on the weekends			
go shopping downtown			

Ask a few students if they like, have, and do the things on the chart. Then have students ask three of their classmates similar yes/no questions, filling in their charts with *yes* and *no*. Last, have students write sentences about their classmates. For example:

Thuy likes American movies.

She doesn't have a driver's license.

2. Bring in blank weekly schedules like the schedule on page 104 of the Student Book, and have students fill in their weekday and weekend activities. Then ask them to exchange schedules with their partners and write eight sentences about their partners' habitual activities. For example:

Makiko goes to work at 4:00 on weekdays.

She swims on Saturday afternoons.

After the students finish writing, have them share some of their sentences with the class.

A. **Read Maria's letter. Then write about her schedule.**

Dear Mom and Dad,   April 16

     I have a new schedule on weekdays. I get up at 6:30 and eat breakfast.
Then I take a shower and get dressed. I don't walk to work any longer
because I don't have time. Now I take the bus. I start work at 8:00. It's
really busy in the morning, but I take a coffee break from 10:00 to 10:15.
Then I work some more. I have lunch around noon. When it's nice outside,
I usually go to a park and eat there. I get off work at 5:00, but I don't get
home until 6:00. I'm usually very tired! So I go to sleep early.

Love,

Maria

Maria has a new schedule on weekdays. She _____

_____

_____

_____

_____

_____

_____

_____

B. **Write a letter to your teacher about your daily schedule.**

Dear _____,   _____

This is my schedule on weekdays. I _____

_____

_____

_____

_____

Sincerely,

_____

UNIT 17 How Often Do You Go Dancing?

Topic: sports and leisure activities

Life Skill/Competency: describing interests

Structure: expressions of frequency

Vocabulary

go dancing	go swimming	take a vacation	football
play cards	exercise	go bowling	soccer
go fishing	eat out	go to church	basketball
watch a movie	take a nap	kiss your husband/wife	volleyball

Teaching Suggestions

Activity 1

Refer to the procedure on page v.

Before beginning the presentation, write *How often?* on the chalkboard and establish its meaning with a few simple examples (e.g., *How often do you go to work?...Every day. How often do you brush your teeth?...Two times a day.*). Then underline the question and below it write the expressions of frequency that appear on page 107 of the Student Book, introducing and clarifying them one by one. Elicit examples of each expression in relation to familiar activities, and leave the expressions on the chalkboard to prompt students during the presentation.

Ask questions like the following to present the pictures.

What's this person doing?

Do you ever _(go dancing)_ ?

How often do you _(go dancing)_ ?

Where do you usually _(go dancing)_ ?

What day do you _(go dancing)_ ?

Who do you _(go dancing)_ with?

The following is a sample presentation of picture 1 (How often do you go dancing?)

> Now we're going to talk about things we do in our leisure time. What's "leisure time"?...Well, we have leisure time on Sunday, or after work...Yes. Leisure time is free time. Now look at this picture. What's this person doing?...Yes, she's dancing. Fanny, how often do you go dancing?...Every Saturday and Sunday? Wow, that's great! Where do you usually go dancing?...Oh, at Disco-land. What about you, Kim, how often do you go dancing?...Not very much. And how about you, Gabriela, how often do you go dancing?

Activity 3

Refer to the procedure on page vii.

After students finish the listening task, call their attention to the fact that the word *family* is singular and takes a singular verb.

Activity 4

When you introduce the expressions of frequency, point out that *once in a while* is similar in meaning to *sometimes*. After the class has repeated all of the expressions, have students practice the expressions orally. First, pantomime some actions, such as *watch TV, clean the house,* and *take a shower.* Have students ask you a yes/no question and a question with *How often...?* For example:

Ss: Are you watching TV?

T: Yes, I am.

Ss: How often do you watch TV?

T Once in a while.

Next, ask individual students questions with *How often...?* and have the rest of the class repeat the answers. For example:

T Chantal, how often do you go shopping?

C: Every Sunday.

T Class, how often does she go shopping?

Ss: She goes shopping every Sunday.

Activity 5

Before students begin the writing task, remind them to capitalize days of the week.

Activity 6

Refer to the procedure on page ix.

Write the question words on the chalkboard before students begin the pairwork.

For reinforcement of question formation, refer to Expansion Activity 1.

Activity 7

After students finish the writing task, have them share their sentences with the class.

Activity 8

If students need additional practice writing the third-person singular form of verbs, put the following list of verbs on the chalkboard and have them add *-s* or *-es*.

dress up	visit	go	catch	exercise
fish	brush	come	shave	have
talk	drive	scratch	cry	yawn

In addition, teach students when to use the long and short endings on third-person singular verbs. First, say these pairs of verbs aloud, clapping out the syllables: *read/reads, play/plays, wait/waits, watch/watches, kiss/kisses,* and *wash/washes.* Go through the pairs of verbs again, having students clap and repeat after you. Then write *Long sound* and *Short sound* at the top of two columns on one side of the chalkboard and the following list of verbs on the other side of the chalkboard.

sleep	teach	meet	swim	relax
visit	play	drive	fix	cry
study	brush	scratch	kiss	wear
yawn	watch	work	wash	like

Point to the verbs one by one and say both the simple form and the third-person singular form. Have students tell you whether both forms of the verb have the same number of syllables or whether the third-person singular form has an extra syllable. Write each verb in the appropriate column. Then circle the verb endings that require an additional syllable: *-ch, -x, -sh,* and *-s.* Explain that when verbs end with /ch/, /j/, /s/, /sh/, /x/, and /z/, the third-person singular form will have an additional syllable. Point to the verbs again and have students pronounce the third-person singular forms.

Activity 10

Refer to the procedure on page x.

As you introduce the new vocabulary items, ask various students if they play these games or watch them on TV.

After students finish the listening task, have them write four complete sentences about each person's sports and leisure activities for homework. For example:

> Pablo doesn't play baseball.

> He plays soccer every Saturday morning.

For reinforcement of sports and leisure activities, refer to Expansion Activity 2.

Expansion Activities

1. For a challenging review of question formation, make a transparency of the following chart and have the students play *Jeopardy*. In addition to this transparency, you'll need 30 counters or squares of paper to cover the answers.

	SHOPPING	WORK	HOUSING	HABITS	SPORTS/ LEISURE
25 POINTS	It's $20.95.	I start work at 7:00.	It's in the bathroom.	No, I don't. I drink tea.	I swim downtown.
50 POINTS	The supermarket is across from the bank.	I go to work by bus.	Yes, there is. It's in the kitchen	I wash the dishes after dinner.	Yes, I do. I play a lot.
75 POINTS	They're 85¢ a can.	I work 8 hours a day.	There are three bedrooms.	I study with my sister.	I run twice a week.
100 POINTS	It's an extra large.	No, I don't. I have a part-time job.	They're in the basement.	I do my laundry once a week.	I go fishing with my dad.
150 POINTS	They're 29¢ each.	I have Sunday off.	No, there aren't.	I watch action movies.	No, I don't. But I watch it on TV.
200 POINTS	They're on the second floor.	I wear casual clothes.	No, it isn't. It's upstairs.	I keep my money at First Bank.	It depends. Sometimes on Saturday, sometimes on Sunday.

To play the game, put the transparency on the overhead projector and cover all the answers with markers before turning on the projector. (If you don't have an overhead projector, the same chart can be drawn on the chalkboard and each question covered with a piece of paper.)

a. Divide the class into two or more teams and number the members of each team.

b. A member of one team chooses a topic and number of points. (The more difficult questions are awarded a greater number of points.)

c. He or she must ask a question that corresponds to the answer for the topic and number of points chosen. If the answer contains the pronouns *it* or *they*, the question should be formulated using an appropriate noun. For example, an appropriate question for *It's on the corner of Third and Polk* might be *Where is the hospital?*

d. If a student asks an appropriate question, his or her team will be awarded the number of points to the left of the question. If a student asks a question that is not appropriate, a member of another team gets a chance to ask a question.

e. Keep score on the chalkboard.

f. When all of the answers have elicited appropriate questions, the game ends. The team with the most points wins.

2. To review sports and leisure activities and expressions of frequency, ask individuals to go to the front of the classroom and mime one recreational activity they participate in. Have the rest of the class ask and answer questions about the activity. For example:

Ss: Are you fishing?

Trung: Yes, I am.

Ss: How often do you go fishing?

Trung: Twice a month.

T: Class, how often does Trung go fishing?

Ss: He goes fishing twice a month.

UNIT 17 EXERCISES

A. Complete the story about Tim's leisure activities. Use the words in the box. Remember to add *-s* or *-es* if necessary. Use each word once.

catch	do	eat	go	have	play	swim	watch

Tim has a lot of leisure activities. After school, he often plays baseball with his friends. On Friday, he _____ in a swimming pool near his house. At night, he usually _____ TV with his sister and brother. Sometimes they _____ cards. On Saturday morning, Tim _____ fishing with his father. They don't usually _____ many fish, but they always _____ a good time. On Sunday, Tim _____ out in a restaurant with his family. In the evening, he _____ his homework and gets ready for school the next day.

B. Look at the pictures on pages 105 and 110 of the Student Book. Write about the sports and leisure activities of members of your family and friends.

Example: *My husband goes bowling every Sunday afternoon.*

1. _____

2. _____

3. _____

4. _____

5. _____

6. _____

7. _____

8. _____

UNIT 18 | What Does Sue Do?

Topic: occupations and duties

Life Skill/Competency: reporting emergencies

Structure: present tense

Vocabulary

police officer—keep the streets safe	dentist—take care of your teeth
fire fighter—put out fires	janitor—clean buildings
mail carrier—deliver the mail	security guard—watch stores
bus driver—drive a bus	mechanic—fix cars
teacher—teach lessons	factory worker—work in a factory
seamstress—sew clothes	fire station stranger
housewife—take care of the house	fire truck car accident
cashier—take your money, give you change	police station ambulance
secretary—work in an office	police car emergency
operator—help with phone calls	cross street
waitress/waiter—serve meals at a restaurant	

Teaching Suggestions
Activity 1

Refer to the procedure on page v.

When you ask what the various people do in their jobs, students' responses (during the presentation and during conversation practice) needn't be restricted to those listed on page 112 of the Student Book. The captions in the book are for students' reference, but appropriate variations or expansions are to be encouraged.

Ask questions like the following to present the pictures.

What is this person's job?

Where does a ___(teacher)___ work?

What does a ___(teacher)___ do?

Do you know a ___(waitress)___?

Are any of you ___(cashiers)___?

What does a ___(mechanic)___ wear?

The following is a sample presentation of Picture 1 (police officer).

> Today we're going to talk about jobs. What's a job?...Yes, it's your work. For example, what's my job?... Yes, I'm a teacher. Now, let's look at this first picture. Who is this?...Yes, it's Sue. And what does Sue do? Is she a police officer, or a teacher?...Yes. She's a police officer...Yes, José, we also say "policeman" and "policewoman." They all have the same meaning. Now tell me, what color are a police officer's clothes?...Yes, a police officer wears blue clothes. And where does a police officer work?...Yes, a police officer works on the street. And what does a police officer do? Does she teach or keep the streets safe?...Yes, she keeps the streets safe. Do you know "safe"?...Yes, Roberto, it's the opposite of "dangerous." And when do you feel safe—during the day or at night?...Yes, me too. I feel safe during the day. And do you feel safe at home, or on a dark street?...Yes. I feel safe at home, too.

Activity 2

Refer to the procedure on page vi.

After students have repeated all of the vocabulary items on this page, go through the verbs a second time, reviewing the pronunciation of third-person singular endings. First, write *Long sound* and *Short sound* at the top of two columns on the chalkboard. One by one, say the simple form of the verbs aloud and have students say whether the third-person singular form has a short ending or a long ending. Write each verb in the appropriate column. Then have students pronounce the third-person singular form of each verb. Last, use each verb in a sentence that students must repeat. For example: *A police officer keeps the streets safe.* Help students pronounce the verb endings correctly.

Activity 3

In your discussion of *A.M.* and *P.M.*, remind students that 12 *A.M.* means *midnight* and 12 *P.M.* means *noon*.

Activity 4

Refer to the procedure on page ix.

After students finish the pairwork, ask them questions about their own jobs and job duties. For example:

T: Ziyi, what do you do?

Z: I'm a seamstress.

T: What do you do at work?

Z: I sew clothes.

T: Class, what does Ziyi do at work?

Ss: She sews clothes.

Activity 5

As you introduce the new vocabulary items, ask students if there are police and fire stations in their neighborhoods. If so, ask where they're located.

Activity 6

After students have read the paragraphs and answered the questions, write two sets of questions on the chalkboard as follows.

If you work	If you don't work
1. What's your name?	1. What's your name?
2. What do you do?	2. What do you do?
3. What hours do you work?	3. What hours do you go to school?
4. Where do you work?	4. Where do you go to school?
5. Do you work the day shift or the night shift?	5. When do you go to school?
6. When do you go to work?	6. When do you leave school?
7. When do you get off work?	7. What do you do at school?
8. What do you do at work?	

Have students respond to all of the questions by writing paragraphs about themselves following the models on page 114 of the Student Book.

For reinforcement of occupations and job duties, refer to Expansion Activities 1 and 2.

Activity 7

Refer to the procedure on page x.

Prepare students for the activities on pages 115 and 116 of the Student Book by asking them when they call 911 for help. List these situations—fire, robbery, accidents—on the chalkboard. Have students describe any personal experiences they may have had with emergency situations.

When you introduce the first vocabulary item, ask several students what streets they live on and what the cross streets are. Have them draw simple diagrams of their houses and the surrounding streets on the chalkboard.

Before listening to the conversations, have students look at the pictures and describe what's happening in each one.

Expansion Activities

1. To review the different occupations, read each of the following short conversations aloud and have students guess the occupation of the significant speaker. To indicate when the speaker changes, use dolls or puppets, or draw two stick figures on the chalkboard and point to them as you speak.

   A: Is there a letter for me?

   B: I'm sorry, ma'am. There's no mail for you today.

   A: Here's the money.

   B: Thank you. Sir! Here's your change!

   A: Can you give me the number for Al's Barber Shop, please?

   B: Yes. The number is 776-9315.

   A: Can you please wash the windows?

   B: Yes, after I finish cleaning the floor.

   A: What's wrong?

   B: My teeth hurt.

   A: Well, open your mouth and let's have a look.

   A: Can you fix this car on Monday?

   B: I'll take a look at it, but I'm not sure I can fix it.

   A: How much is the fare, sir?

   B: It's $1.25.

   A: Where can I put these papers?

   B: Put them on my desk. I'll look at them tomorrow.

   A: What shift do you work?

   B: The night shift. I get home from the factory at 6 A.M.

   A: What do you have to drink?

   B: Coffee and tea, sir.

   A: Bring me some coffee, please.

2. To review the occupations further, bring in a set of flashcards (which you have made before class) with the names of the occupations. Give students the cards and have them take turns going to the front of the classroom and miming their occupations. Have the class guess the occupations and practice talking about job duties by asking questions. For example:

Ss: Are you a janitor?

S: No, I'm not.

Ss: Are you a mechanic?

S: Yes, I am.

Ss: Do you fix cars?

S: Yes, I do.

UNIT 18 EXERCISES

A. Write the missing words.

1. A seamstress _____sews_____ clothes.

2. A mechanic _____ cars.

3. A _____ puts out fires.

4. A janitor _____ buildings.

5. An _____ helps with phone calls.

6. A _____ takes your money and gives you change.

7. A security guard _____ stores.

8. A _____ takes care of the house.

9. A mail carrier _____ the mail.

10. A _____ works in a factory.

B. The sentences in this conversation are not in the correct order. Number the sentences correctly and write the conversation below.

_____ OK, Ms. Fisher. A police car is on the way.

_____ 806 Park Avenue.

_____ What's your name?

_____ Hello. I need help. There's a stranger in my garage.

_____ Nancy Fisher.

___1___ 911 Emergency.

_____ What's your address?

A: **911 Emergency.**

B: _____

A: _____

B: _____

A: _____

B: _____

A: _____

UNIT 19 Your Family

Topic: family tree

Life Skill/Competency: postal services

Structure: present tense

Vocabulary

husband	son	granddaughter	uncle	aerogram
wife	brother	grandson	aunt	money order
father	sister	nephew	cousin	package
mother	grandfather	niece	stamp	airmail
daughter	grandmother			

Teaching Suggestions
Activity 1

Refer to the procedure on page v.

The vocabulary of family relationships is generally taught at the literacy level. Use the captioned family tree on the first page of the unit to review and clarify that vocabulary. Start with "me" (in the middle of the page) and ask questions like the following to present the family tree.

Who is this person?

Do you have a ____(sister)____?

How many ___(sisters)___ do you have?

What is/are your ___(sister's)___ name(s)?

How old is/are your ___(sister)___?

Where do(es) your ___(sisters)___ live?

The following is a sample presentation of *husband, wife,* and *children.*

> Today we're going to talk about people in our family. Let's start with "me." Here [pointing]—do you see "me"? And this [pointing] is my husband—or wife, if I'm a man. This fat line [pointing] shows that we're married. Now you see we have one daughter [pointing] and one son [pointing]. What's a daughter?... Yes, a girl. And a son?...Yes, a son is a boy. So how many children do we have?...Yes, we have two children. What are children?...Yes, children are sons and daughters. Now, Lee, how many sons do you have?...Oh, one son. And how many daughters?...Yes, two daughters. So, class, how many children does Lee have?...Yes, he has three children.

Activity 3

After students finish the writing task, have them read the sentences aloud, reminding them to use falling intonation and helping them with the pronunciation of the 's on the possessive nouns. If students are omitting /s/ or /z/, show them how to practice more slowly, drawing out the possessive endings, until they can pronounce the sentences correctly at normal speed.

To review the family terms, have students take out a piece of paper and make three columns. Then dictate the kinship terms one by one and have students write them in the first column. In the second column, have students write the number of people in their family who fall into that category (e.g., how many nieces they have, how many uncles). In the third column, have students write where their relatives live. Finally, have them share some of this information with the class. For example:

> I have two aunts. They live in China.

> I have three sisters. One lives in Mexico and the others live in the United States.

Activity 4

Point out "Jody" in the middle of the page and, choosing her relatives in random order, ask these questions about each person.

> What is Jody's __(uncle's)__ name?

> What does Jody's __(uncle)__ do?

Activity 6

After practicing the conversation with the students, write these question cues on the chalkboard: *name, where live, job.* Following the model conversation, ask several students about members of their families and have the class ask you about your family. Then start the pairwork.

For reinforcement of family terms, refer to Expansion Activities 1, 2, and 3.

Activity 7

Refer to the procedure on page x.

Prepare students for the activities on pages 121 and 122 of the Student Book by asking these questions.

> *Is there a post office in your neighborhood?;*

> *Where is it?; When does it open? When does it close?;*

> *Is it open on Saturdays?; Do you go to the post office? Why?*

As you introduce the vocabulary items, ask students if and when they buy or send these items and how much they cost.

Before listening to the conversations, have students describe what's happening in each of the four pictures.

Activity 9

As you talk about the money order with the students, tell them the post office is responsible for printing the amount on the money order. Show them where the amount will appear.

For reinforcement of language related to postal services, refer to Expansion Activity 4.

Expansion Activities

1. To review family relationships, make two columns on the chalkboard, one labeled *males* and the other labeled *females.* Hold up flashcards (which you have made before class) with the kinship terms. Have students read the words and say which category they belong to. Tape each flashcard to the chalkboard in the correct column.

2. Have students draw and label their own family trees following the model on page 117 of the Student Book. Ask students to label and name all of the members in their families. When students have finished their drawings, ask them to count their living relatives and find out who has the biggest family.

3. Dictate the following short paragraph about Jody's sister and have students write it in their notebooks. Then have students write short paragraphs about two of their family members, following the model.

   My sister's name is Jane. She's 53 years old. She lives in New York. She's a secretary. She works in an office. She writes letters. She answers the telephone too.

4. Bring in items from the post office—stamps, aerograms, money orders, and packages—and set up a post office in the classroom. Review the vocabulary items and write the following cues on the chalkboard.

Stamps/Aerograms	Packages	Money Orders
Can I help you?	Can I help you?	Can I help you?
OK. Anything else?	Airmail?	For how much?
That's $_____.	OK. Anything else?	OK. Anything else?
Thank you.	That's $_____.	That's $_____.
	Thank you.	Thank you.

For each item, improvise a conversation. First, have the class take the part of the mail clerk and you take the part of the customer. Then switch roles. Go through each dialogue twice. Then erase all but the first word in each utterance. Ask pairs of students to go to the front of the classroom and role-play the conversations.

UNIT 19 EXERCISES

A. **Look at the picture of Jody's family on page 119. Write the missing words.**

1. Jody's aunt is a _____*housewife*_____. ____*She's*____ 74.

2. Jody's husband is a _____. _____ 56.

3. Jody's _____ is a bus driver. _____ 37.

4. Jody's sister is a_____. _____ 53.

5. Jody's _____ is a mechanic. _____ 18.

6. Jody's mother is a _____. _____ 75.

7. Jody's_____ is a janitor. _____ 32.

8. Jody's grandmother is an_____. _____ 98.

9. Jody's uncle is a_____. _____ 73.

10. Jody's_____is a fire fighter. _____ 52.

B. **Read about Stan and Maria's families. Then answer the questions.**

Stan's family is different from Maria's family. Everyone in Stan's family lives in the United States. Some people in Maria's family live in the United States, but other family members live in Mexico. Both of Stan's grandmothers and grandfathers live in California. Maria's mother's parents live in California too, but her father's parents aren't living. Stan's only brother is single. He doesn't have any sisters. Maria has two brothers and four sisters. Three of Maria's sisters are married and have children. Stan has one aunt and two uncles. The aunt is married, and she has a daughter. Both of the uncles are single. Maria has twelve aunts and uncles. All of the aunts and uncles are married and have children. Stan and Maria come from very different families, but they like each other a lot.

1. Who has family in Mexico?   *Maria does.*_____

2. Who has four grandparents?   _____

3. Who has a small family?   _____

4. Who has nieces and nephews?   _____

5. Who has lots of cousins?   _____

UNIT 20 | What Do They Do? What Are They Doing?

Topic: vacation activities

Life Skill/Competency: first aid

Structure: present tense versus present continuous tense

Vocabulary				
ride horses	spaghetti	cut	the chills	cream
camp	seafood	burn	Band-Aid	blanket
play golf	barbecued hamburgers	bee sting	ice	

Teaching Suggestions
Activity 1

Refer to the procedure on page v.

This unit contrasts present tense ("most summers") with present continuous tense ("this summer"). The students will be producing statements during the presentation, as in the example below. Allow several students to produce each of the statements, and allow extra time for this presentation. Ask the following questions to present each picture.

1. The kids: most summers
   a. What do they usually do?   (Ride horses.)
   b. Where do they ride horses?   (At summer camp.)
   c. How long do they stay at camp?   (Three weeks.)
   d. Who do they go to camp with?   (Their classmates.)
   e. What kind of food do they eat there?   (Terrible food.)

2. The kids: this summer
   a. What are they doing?   (Camping.)
   b. Where are they camping?   (In Alaska.)
   c. How long are they staying in Alaska?   (Two weeks.)
   d. Who are they going with?   (Their parents.)
   e. What kind of food are they eating?   (Barbecued hamburgers.)

3. Stan: most summers
   a. What does he usually do in the summer?   (Relaxes.)
   b. Where does he relax?   (At his mother's house.)
   c. How long does he stay there?   (One month.)
   d. Who does he go with?   (His sister.)
   e. What kind of food does he eat there?   (Spaghetti.)

4. Stan: this summer
   a. What's he doing?   (Playing golf.)
   b. Where is he playing golf?   (In Hawaii.)
   c. How long is he staying in Hawaii?   (Ten days.)
   d. Who is he going with?   (Nobody./He's alone.)
   e. What kind of food is he eating?   (Seafood.)

The following is a sample presentation of Picture 1 (the kids at summer camp).

> Today we're going to talk about summer activities. Who are these people [pointing]?...Yes, the kids, Tim and Kate. And this first group of pictures [indicating] is what the kids do most summers [pointing to the words "most summers"]. What does that mean, "most summers"?...Yes, it means "usually." Now, what do the kids usually do in the summer? Do they drive cars, or ride horses?...Yes. They ride horses. What's a horse?...Yes, it's an animal. Where do the kids ride horses, at home, or at summer camp?... Yes. At summer camp [pointing to picture]. What's a summer camp?...Yes, it's in the summer. And do kids go to summer camp to study?...No way. They go to have fun. What do they do at summer camp?... Yes, they swim. What else do they do at summer camp?...Yes, they play baseball. Okay, and how long do Tim and Kate stay at camp [pointing to dates]?... Yes, they stay for three weeks. And who do they go with, their parents or their classmates?...Yes, they go with their classmates. Now, what kind of food do they eat? Do they eat good food [pointing to picture]?...No! They eat terrible food! What's "terrible"?... Yes, terrible means very, very bad. Now, look at the picture and listen. [Slowly, pointing to individual parts of picture:] Most summers the kids ride horses at summer camp for three weeks. They go with their classmates and eat terrible food. Now who can say that?... Ulises, do you want to try? Go ahead.

Activity 2

Explain that the procedure for the pairwork is different in this unit. *Both* students look at the pictures on page 123 of the Student Book. Student A attempts to produce a complete sentence. Student B listens and helps out. Then Student A listens while Student B says the sentences.

Activity 3

Before starting the activity, list these *Wh-* words on the chalkboard: *what, where, how long, what kind,* and *who...with.* Point to the relevant expression as you lead the students through the activity.

Activity 5

After practicing the conversations with the students, write these time expressions on the chalkboard: *most weekends/this weekend, most evenings/this evening, most summers/this summer.* Following the model conversations, ask several students about their plans and activities. Next, have the class ask about your plans and activities. After students have made several conversations with a partner, have students share some of the information they've learned about their partners with the class.

For further practice in contrasting the simple present and present continuous tenses, refer to Expansion Activity 1.

Activities 6 and 7

Refer to the procedure on page x.

Prepare students for the activities on pages 127 and 128 of the Student Book by asking these questions.

> *What is first aid?; When do you use it?*

After students finish the listening task in Activity 7, have them write complete sentences about each person's problem. For example: *Tim has the chills.*

Activity 8

As you introduce the new vocabulary, ask students if and when they use these items and where you can buy or get them.

After students have listened to the conversations and filled in the blanks, write the first conversation on the chalkboard. Say it aloud line by line, asking students whether your voice goes up or down at the end of each utterance. Mark the intonation patterns with rising and falling arrows. Point out that when people repeat part of a sentence to verify they've heard it correctly, they use rising intonation. The dialogue will look as follows.

A: I have a cut on my finger.↘

B: A cut?↗ You need a Band-Aid.↘

A: Yeah.↘ Can you please get me one?↗

B: Sure.↘

Practice the two conversations with the students, helping them with intonation.

Activity 9

After students finish the writing task, do a quick review of first aid vocabulary. Tell students about problems you have and have the class tell you what you need to solve them. For example:

T: I have a burn on my leg.

Ss: You need ice.

You may also ask students to volunteer information on various home remedies they use to treat bee stings, cuts, burns, and chills.

For reinforcement of first aid vocabulary, refer to Expansion Activity 2.

Expansion Activities

1. To give students additional practice contrasting the simple present and present continuous tenses, dictate the following separate sets of questions and have students write them in their notebooks.

    What do you do most weekends?; Where do you do it?;
    How long do you do it?; Who do you do it with?

    What are you doing this weekend?; Where are you doing it?
    How long are you doing it?; Who are you doing it with?

    Ask students to write two short paragraphs, one about their habitual activities and the other about their plans. The first should begin with *Most weekends, I...* and include information relating to the first four questions. The second paragraph should begin with *This weekend, I'm...* and include information relating to the last four questions. After students finish, have them share their paragraphs with the class or hand them in.

2. Have students review and practice using the first aid vocabulary by identifying first aid items and using them in role-plays. Put Band-Aids, an ice pack, cream, and a blanket on a desk or table at the front of the classroom. Review the model conversations on page 128 of the Student Book. Then ask pairs of students to go to the front of the classroom. Have them talk about first aid problems and offer each other appropriate items for relief.

A. **Write the missing words. Use the words in the box. Then match the questions and answers.**

is	are	does	do

1. Where _____ they going now? ———— Three days.

2. When _____ she usually ride horses? Love stories.

3. What kind of clothes _____ you wear? A five-minute drive.

4. Who _____ he talking to now? By bus.

5. How far _____ it from your house? On the weekend.

6. Where _____ you get your hair cut? To the movies.

7. What kind of books _____ she read? His boss.

8. What time _____ we leaving tonight? At Mimi's Hair Salon.

9. How _____ he get to work? Casual clothes.

10. How long _____ you staying in Reno? At 10:00.

B. **Complete the story about Tim, Kate, and Baby Ben. Write the correct form of the words in the box. Use each word once.**

do	fish	have	like	play
read	run	stay	swim	watch

Most summers, Tim and Kate ride horses at summer camp for three weeks.

They _____ horses a lot. They _____ other things at camp

too. Tim _____ in Lake Mabel every day, and Kate _____

volleyball. Baby Ben is too young to go to summer camp, so he _____

home with his mother. He plays with Zabu and sometimes he _____ TV.

This summer, all three children are camping in Alaska for two weeks with

their parents. Tim _____ with his father now. He likes fishing a lot.

Kate and Baby Ben _____ around the trees with Zabu. May

_____ a book. They _____ a wonderful time.

UNIT 21 | At the Doctor

Topic: body parts

Life Skill/Competency: making/registering for doctor's appointments, medical checkup, medical history form

Structure: imperatives

Vocabulary

forehead	mouth	head	bottom	scratch	lower
eye	chest	arm	hand	cover	bend
nose	stomach	neck	leg	rub	straighten
lip	finger	shoulder	toe	take off	lie
ear	knee	back	foot/feet	raise/lift	breathe
face	hair	waist	touch		

Teaching Suggestions

Activity 1

The vocabulary in this unit will be reinforced by having students respond physically to commands from you (i.e., through TPR [Total Physical Response]), rather than through picture-based conversation practice. Thus the pictures on pages 129 and 133 of the Student Book appear with captions.

Activity 2

Introduce the four verbs at the top of the page: *touch, scratch, cover,* and *rub*. Have the students close their books, stand, and respond to commands from you that combine these four verbs and the body parts from the first page. For example: *Touch your forehead, Scratch your nose.* After finishing the activity, give students additional practice with the vocabulary for body parts and the four verbs by performing the actions yourself and having the class say what you're doing. For example:

T: What am I doing?

Ss: You're rubbing your shoulder.

Activity 3

For reinforcement of all body parts, refer to Expansion Activity 1.

Activity 4

Refer to the procedure on page ix.

As students look at the picture, ask these questions.

Who's in this picture?; What's he doing?;

Who's he talking to?; How is he feeling?; What's wrong?

After practicing the conversation with the students, write this cue on the chalkboard: *My _____ hurts.* Mime various aches and pains—in the stomach, the head, the shoulder, the leg, the arm, and so on—and have students say what hurts.

Activity 7

Before students begin filling out the form, teach the words *height* and *weight*. First, ask individual students how tall they are and how much they weigh. (Weight may be a sensitive subject for some students, so avoid asking students who might feel embarrassed about how much they weigh.) Some students may volunteer their height and weight using metric terms. Put the terms *meter*, *gram*, and *kilogram* on the chalkboard and explain that in the United States, we use a different system. Write the words *feet* and *inches* on the chalkboard and the following metric equivalents: *1 meter = 39 inches* and *1 meter = 3 feet 3 inches*. Explain how *feet* and *inches* are abbreviated: *five feet four inches* is written *5'4"*. Put several abbreviated heights on the chalkboard and have students read them aloud. Then write the word *pound* on the chalkboard and the following metric equivalents: *1 pound = 454 grams* and *1 kilogram = 2.2 pounds*. If possible, have a bathroom scale available for students to weigh themselves on. In addition, put some type of measuring device on the wall to measure how tall students are.

In addition, teach the word *medicine* by bringing in a few medicine bottles and asking students if they take medicine and, if so, what kind of medicine they take.

For reinforcement and expansion of vocabulary related to medical checkups, refer to Expansion Activity 2.

Activity 8

Introduce the vocabulary on this page by giving TPR commands *before* the students look at the page. Start by telling the students that you are (taking the role of) the doctor, and they are patients at a checkup. Then have them stand and respond as you give the commands. Advance through the page slowly, item by item, and use simple variations to reinforce the verbs. For example: *Take off your shirt/hat/ shoes. Straighten your arm/leg/back.* (Model pantomimed responses for such commands as *Take off your shirt* and *Lie on your stomach.*) Then have students open their books to page 133 as you review the new vocabulary with them.

In addition, use these commands to review stress and rhythm. First, write the commands on the chalkboard. Then model them one by one and have students tell you which syllables are stressed. Mark the stressed syllables with a dot.

Open wide.   Say "Ahhhh!"   Take off your shirt.

Ask students to clap the rhythm of each command. If students need help getting started, show them how to do it, clapping hard on stressed syllables and softly and quickly on unstressed syllables. After students clap the rhythm of each command correctly, have them practice saying it aloud. Call their attention to the fact that the vowel sound in the word *your* is reduced. Thus, when spoken quickly it sounds like *yur*. Go through all of the commands again, saying them quickly and clapping only on the stressed syllables. Have students repeat after you.

Activity 9

Have students stand and follow your commands. (As an alternative, you can have students work in pairs, one reading the commands from page 133 in the Student Book and the other standing and responding.)

Activity 10

For reinforcement of the commands, refer to Expansion Activities 3 and 4.

Expansion Activities

1. To review the vocabulary for body parts, pass out copies of an outline of a human figure to all students. Dictate the parts of the body and have students write the words in the appropriate spots on the diagram.

2. Initiate a class discussion of what it's like to see the doctor in students' native countries. Ask these questions:

   What kind of doctors do you see in your country?; Where do you see them?

In your country, do you see doctors only when you're sick, or do you have regular checkups even when you're healthy?;

How often do you see the doctor for a checkup?;

How are medical checkups in your country different from checkups in the U.S.?;

Who pays the doctor?; Is it expensive to see a doctor in your country?

3. After students finish the listening task in Activity 10, play the following game to review medical commands further. Ask six students to go to the front of the classroom. Have the rest of the class take turns giving them commands. Students who follow the commands correctly remain in the game, but students who make a mistake must return to their seats. The last student to remain standing wins the game. The game may be repeated as many times as necessary to involve all of the students in the class.

4. For a further review of body parts and commands, have the class play Body Part Bingo. (The only thing you'll need to prepare or provide is lots of little paper squares, counters, or coins that students can use to cover up the squares on their bingo cards, which they will make in class.)

Have each student draw a grid that is five squares across and five squares down. Put the following verbs on the chalkboard: *touch, cover, scratch, rub, raise, lower, bend,* and *straighten.* Tell students to choose *five* of these verbs and write one above each of the five columns on their bingo cards. Next, have them fill in the squares on their cards with names of body parts that could be used with each verb. For example, in the column under *straighten,* a student could write *finger, arm, leg, back,* and *shoulder.* You may need to demonstrate this by drawing a sample bingo card on the chalkboard. When the bingo cards are finished, begin the game. Call out commands, such as *Raise your arm* and *Scratch your back.* The first student to get five commands in a row or on the diagonal wins the game. Prizes may be awarded, but be sure to keep track of all of the commands you've called out so you can verify that the winner has indeed won the game.

A. Look at the picture on page 129. Write the body parts in the correct column.

HEAD	MIDDLE	ARM	LEG
face	*stomach*		
hair			

B. Match the parts of the sentences.

1.	Raise your	"Ahhhh!"
2.	Hold your	arm.
3.	Bend your	mouth.
4.	Say	stomach.
5.	Breathe	breath.
6.	Open your	shirt.
7.	Take off your	knee.
8.	Straighten your	in.
9.	Lie on your	leg.

UNIT 22 | What's the Matter with May?

Topic: health problems

Life Skill/Competency: medicines

Structure: present tense

Vocabulary

headache	fever/temperature	thermometer
toothache	cough	aspirin
earache	sore throat	diarrhea medicine
stomachache	rash	antacid
backache	diarrhea	cough syrup
cold/flu	dizzy	

Teaching Suggestions

Activity 1

Refer to the procedure on page v.

As in Unit 4, students will be asked a question during the presentation that is not answered in the book: *Why does this person have this problem?* They are to speculate freely.

Ask questions like the following to present the pictures.

What's the matter with this person?

How do you know he/she has a (headache) ?

Why does he/she have a (headache) ?

Do you ever get a (headache) ?

Why/When do you have a   (headache) ?

What do you do when you have a (headache) ?

The following is a sample presentation of Picture 1 (a headache).

> Today we're going to talk about when we're not feeling well. What does that mean—"not feeling well"?...
> Yes, it means we're sick, we have a problem with our body. And when someone isn't feeling well, we can ask them, "What's the matter?" For example, let's take a look at May here. Is May feeling well?...No, she isn't. Well then, what's the matter with May?...Yes, her head hurts. Or, we can say she has a headache. How do you know she has a headache?...Yes, she's touching her forehead. Now why do you think she has a headache? Any ideas?...You think she's been working too hard, Fernando? Well, that's one reason people get headaches. Any other ideas?...Yes, Zoe, maybe she has a headache because she has a cold. Do you ever get headaches?...You do sometimes, Ali?

Activity 2

Refer to the procedure on page vi.

After students finish the pairwork, give them more practice with the new vocabulary. Say a series of sentences, such as *You have a fever* and *You feel dizzy*, and have students mime the ailments at their seats. Then mime the ailments yourself and have students say what's wrong.

Activity 5

Refer to the procedure on page ix.

Before practicing the conversations with the students, explain that *since* must be followed by an expression that refers to some time in the past. Put these cues on the chalkboard.

Since	
	Friday
	this morning
	last night
	yesterday
	October 1

Activity 6

Before students start the pairwork, read the first question aloud and elicit a few responses from the class as a whole. Remind students that their answers will begin with the word *because*.

After students finish the pairwork, have them share their answers with the class. Students' answers may not be perfectly grammatical, but teachers are advised to correct minimally and only when the meaning is unclear.

For reinforcement of health problems, refer to Expansion Activity 1.

Activity 7

Prepare students for the activities on page 139 of the Student Book by asking these questions.

When do you take your temperature?; Who takes your temperature?;

Do you have a thermometer?; Do people in your country use thermometers?

Discuss the difference between Celsius and Fahrenheit. Explain that while most thermometers sold in the United States have both scales, doctors and nurses will report temperatures in degrees Fahrenheit.

Activity 9

Refer to the procedure on page x.

As you introduce the vocabulary items, have actual medicine bottles on hand to pass around so that students can look at them, open them, and smell the contents. Ask students if and when they use these medicines.

Use the dialogue to review stress and intonation. As students are listening to the conversation, write it on the chalkboard. Then model it line by line. Ask students which word is the loudest in each sentence and whether your voice goes up or down at the end of each utterance. Mark the primary stress with a dot and the intonation with rising and falling arrows. Remind students that when they repeat part of a sentence to verify they've heard it correctly, they should use rising intonation. The dialogue will look as follows.

A: I'm not feeling well.

B: What's the problem?

A: I have a headache.

B: Why don't you take some aspirin?

A: Aspirin? That's a good idea.

Practice the dialogue with the students, helping them with stress and intonation.

Activity 10

After students finish the pairwork, ask them what medications and remedies they use in their countries to treat the ailments introduced in this unit. Make a list of these remedies on the chalkboard. Then have students work in pairs to write two dialogues about health problems in which they suggest remedies or medications that they might recommend to a friend. Have them perform their dialogues for the class.

For reinforcement of medicines and medical advice, refer to Expansion Activities 2 and 3.

Expansion Activities

1. To review health problems, give each student a flashcard (which you have made before class) with the name of one of the illnesses. Have students mime their problems in front of the class. The rest of the class must say what's wrong. For example:

   T: What's the matter with Heidi?

   Ss: She has a sore throat.

2. To give students more practice talking about health problems and offering medical advice, engage the class in dialogues following the model conversation on page 140 of the Student Book. Review the medicines on this page and bring in and introduce the vocabulary for other over-the-counter medications such as throat lozenges and Tylenol. Initiate dialogues about health problems that can be alleviated in various ways, and encourage students to give advice based on their own experience. For example:

   T: Ophelia, I'm not feeling well.

   O: What's the problem?

   T: I have a sore throat.

   O: Why don't you drink some lemon tea?

   T: Lemon tea? That's a good idea.

   After you've elicited advice from several students, have students continue the practice working in pairs.

3. Ask students to visit a local drug store to gather information about the location and price of thermometers and the medications introduced in this unit. For homework, have them write two sentences about each item. For example:

   The cough syrup is on aisle 7. It's $3.29 a bottle.

UNIT 22 EXERCISES

A. Write the missing words. Use the words in the box.

is	has	hurts	feels
are	have	hurt	feel

1. I _____ a sore throat.

2. My arm _____ .

3. He _____ dizzy.

4. Her feet _____.

5. The baby _____ a cold.

6. The kids _____ sick in bed.

7. They _____ dizzy.

8. My legs _____ .

9. His head _____.

10. You _____ a fever.

11. She _____ tired all the time.

12. He _____ diarrhea.

13. My teeth _____.

14 He _____ sick today.

15. You _____ a rash.

16. She _____ the flu.

B. Read the health problems and complete the conversations.

1. A: I have a headache.

   B: _Why don't you take some aspirin?_ _____

2. A: I have a cough.

   B: _____

3. A: I have diarrhea.

   B: _____

4. A: My stomach hurts.

   B: _____

5. A: My temperature is 102°.

   B: _____

UNIT 23 | What's Maria Going to Do Tomorrow?

Topic: future plans

Life Skills/Competencies: personal care; the calendar

Structure: future *going to*

Vocabulary

pack	play golf	unpack	comb hair	razor
fly to Alaska	climb a mountain	see Stan	wash hair	comb
ride a horse	play tennis	brush teeth	dry hair	shampoo
go fishing	fly back	shave	toothbrush	hair dryer

Teaching Suggestions
Activity 1

Refer to the procedure on page v.

Proceed from one picture to the next (in the calendar) using the expression, *the next day*. Do not introduce the time expressions on page 143 of the Student Book until after the vocabulary on page 142 has been introduced and practiced. The future *going to* will be used in the presentation, but not formally introduced until page 144.

Ask questions like the following to present the pictures.

What's Maria going to do the next day?

When do we (pack a suitcase) ?

Where do we (play tennis) ?

Do/Did you ever (climb a mountain) ?

When do/did you (play tennis) ?

Who do/did you (play golf) with?

How often do you (go fishing) ?

The following is a sample presentation of Picture 1 (pack).

> Today we're going to talk about Maria's summer plans. First, what do we have here?...Yes, it's a calendar. Is there a calendar in this room? Where is it? Point to it...Yes, that's the calendar over there. Now, back to this calendar, what month is it?...Yes, it's July. And what day is today?...Yes, today is July 10th. And Maria is going to take a trip this summer. What's a "trip"?...Yes, when you go away somewhere. Who took a trip last summer?...Oh, Julio, where did you take a trip to?...Disneyland? Well, Maria's going to take a trip to Alaska. You know where Alaska is [indicating classroom map of the United States]?... Yes, it's there [pointing on map]. What's Maria going to do tomorrow [indicating on calendar]?...Is she going to go fishing, or pack?...Yes, she's going to pack. What's this [pointing to suitcase]?...Yes, it's a suitcase. When do we use a suitcase?...Yes, when we take a trip. Do you have a suitcase, Anton?...You do? What color is your suitcase?... Brown? Oh, same as mine! Now then, what's Maria going to pack in her suitcase?...Yes, her clothes. What else is she going to pack?...Yes, her toothbrush. So tomorrow Maria's going to pack. And what's she going to do the next day?

Activity 4

To prepare students for this activity, have them look at the calendar on page 143 of the Student Book and tell you what month it is. Then say a series of dates and have students say the corresponding days of the week. For example:

> T: July 3.
>
> Ss: Tuesday.

Last, make reference to a series of days and have students say the corresponding dates. For example:

> T: The second Monday.
>
> Ss: July 9.

Activity 5

Refer to the procedure on page vii.

After students finish the Listen and Write activity, have them close their books and look at a large calendar at the front of the classroom. Ask them to tell you the current day, month, and date. Then reinforce the future time expressions by pointing to various future dates and asking three students what they're going to do at that time. Have them respond with short answers. For example:

> T: Monique, what are you going to do three days from now?
>
> M: Relax at home.

Grammar Boxes   (page 144 of Student Book)

Refer to the procedure on page viii.

Point out that the short answer to the first question—*What's she doing tomorrow?*—is *Packing a suitcase*, and the short answer to the second question—*What's she going to do tomorrow?*—is *Pack a suitcase*.

Refer to a current calendar. Point to various future times on the calendar and ask individual students what they're going to do on that day. Have half of the class transform your questions into the third-person singular and the other half of the class repeat the answers. For example:

> T: (pointing to Saturday) What are you going to do on Saturday, Linda?
>
> L: Do the laundry.
>
> Ss1: What's she going to do on Saturday?
>
> Ss2: Do the laundry.

Activity 6

Refer to the procedure on page ix.

As you practice the conversations with the students, teach them the pronunciation of *going to* in informal spoken English. Write these two questions on the chalkboard: *What's Maria going to do this Friday?* and *What's she going to do next Thursday?* Cross out the words *going to* and above them write *gunna*. Explain that *going to* is often pronounced *gunna* in informal speech. Have students repeat the sentences using *gunna*. Then say these time expressions one by one—*tomorrow, this Friday, next week, four days from now, the day after tomorrow, in ten days, this weekend, next month*—and have students produce questions. For example:

> What's she *gunna* do tomorrow?
>
> What's she *gunna* do this Friday?

Encourage students to practice both ways of pronouncing *going to* as they do the pairwork.

Activity 7

After you practice the conversations with the students, refer to a current calendar. As you point to various future times, have students ask you questions about what you're going to do at those times. Then ask several students about their plans.

After students finish interviewing their classmates, have them share some of the information they've gathered with the class.

To reinforce the future with *going to*, refer to Expansion Activity 1.

Activity 8

Refer to the procedure on page x.

As you introduce the new vocabulary, ask students when and how often they do these personal chores.

Activity 9

As you introduce the new vocabulary, ask students if they have these things and what color/kind they have/use.

To reinforce the vocabulary for personal care, refer to Expansion Activity 2.

Expansion Activities

1. Put students into groups of four or five and have them plan a weeklong vacation. Pick a week in the near future and pass out copies of a current calendar with that week set off in brackets. Then show students a world map and tell them to choose a place to go, anywhere in the world. To spark their imaginations, ask several students where they'd like to go and talk a little bit about the climate, terrain, and culture of the places they mention.

    Then have them start working in groups to decide where they want to go and what they want to do on every day of the week. (Remind them not to forget about travel time.) Have all group members enter these activities on their calendars.

    After students finish planning their vacations, have students from different groups ask each other where they're going and what they're going to do on the various days of the week. To end the activity, ask the class which group they think has planned the most exciting vacation.

2. To review the vocabulary for personal care, dictate the toiletry items from page 146 of the Student Book and have students draw pictures and label them. Beside each item, have students write what it's used for.

A. Make a calendar for this month. Write the name of the month and number the days.

SUN.	MON.	TUES.	WED.	THURS.	FRI.	SAT.

Now write the dates.

1. tomorrow _____

2. four days from now _____

3. in two weeks _____

4. this Sunday _____

5. a week from Friday _____

6. next Monday _____

7. in ten days _____

8. the day after tomorrow _____

B. Write questions beginning with *what*.

1. you/this Friday _*What are you going to do this Friday?*_

2. your mother/next week _____

3. you/the day after tomorrow _____

4. your son/a week from Monday _____

5. the kids/next summer _____

UNIT 24 | What's Going to Happen Next Monday?

Topic: predictions

Life Skill/Competency: requesting time off work

Structure: future *going to*

Vocabulary

get a ring	buy a car	get in trouble
get married	take the bus	eat all day
go to work	make a mess	sleep all day
get a raise	clean (their) room	not do anything

Teaching Suggestions

Activity 1

Refer to the procedure on page v.

Ask questions like the following to present the pictures.

What's ___(Maria)___ going to do on ___(Monday)___?

(What's going to happen to ___Maria___ on ___Monday___?)

Why is/isn't he/she going to _(take the bus)_?

(Why are/aren't they going to _take the bus_?)

Do/Did you ever _(buy a new car)_?

When did you _(buy a new car)_?

Do you like/want to _(sleep all day)_?

The following is a sample presentation of what Maria is going to do next week.

> Today John and Maria are talking to a fortune-teller [indicating the fortune-teller in the picture]. Do you know what a fortune-teller is?...Yes. She tells you about your future. For example, what does she tell you?... Yes, if you're going to get married. And...? Yes, if you're going to make a lot of money. Do you ever go to a fortune teller?...You do, Juana?...And you don't, Tamim? So you don't believe in fortune-tellers? Well, let's see what this fortune-teller is saying. First let's look at Maria's fortune. What's going to happen to Maria next Monday [indicating in picture]?...Yes, she's going to get a ring! Does anyone here have a ring?...Yes, you have a ring, Sally, and you have a ring, Rubens. Where do we wear rings, class?...Yes, we wear rings on our fingers. Now, what sometimes happens after someone gets a ring?...Yes, they get married. In fact, what's going to happen to Maria on Tuesday?...Sure enough! She's going to get married! And what about Wednesday? Is she going to go to work [indicating the big **X** in picture]?...No, she isn't. She isn't going to go to work the day after she gets married. Why isn't she going to go to work?...Yes, I suppose she will be on a honeymoon with her husband. Now let's see what's going to happen to John next week.

Grammar Box (page 149 of Student Book)

Refer to the procedure on page viii.

Have four students go to the chalkboard and write their names and their weekly work schedules. For example:

> Mon.: 3 – 11 P.M.
>
> Tues.: day off
>
> Wed.: 3 – 11 P.M. (etc.)

Have the class make affirmative and negative statements based on these schedules and the verbal cues that you supply. Encourage them to practice using *gunna*. For example:

> T: Monday, Roberto.
>
> Ss: He's *gunna* work this Monday.
>
> T: Saturday, Thuy and Paula.
>
> Ss: They aren't *gunna* work this Saturday.

Grammar Box (page 150 of Student Book)

Refer to the procedure on page viii.

Give students verbal cues and have them make sentences about what they are and aren't going to do next week. For example:

> T Clean the house, Jaime.
>
> J: I'm going to clean the house next week.
>
> T: Do my laundry, Sandra.
>
> S: I'm not going to do my laundry next week.

Activity 6

After students finish the writing task, have them share some sentences with the class.

For reinforcement of *going to*, refer to Expansion Activities 1 and 2.

Activities 7 and 8

Refer to the procedure on page x.

Prepare students for the activities on page 151 of the Student Book by asking these questions.

> *Are there times when you can't go to work? Why?;*
>
> *Who do you talk to when you can't go to work?;*
>
> *What do you say?; Does your boss always say yes?*

Activity 9

Before students do the dialogue completion, have them look at each picture and describe what's going on.

Activity 10

After students practice their dialogues with their partners, have a few pairs of students perform their dialogues for the class.

For further practice asking for time off, refer to Expansion Activity 3.

Expansion Activities

1. To review *going to* and future time expressions, play a game in which three students assume the role of fortune-teller. First, list these time expressions on the chalkboard: *this summer, next year, three years from now*. Then ask three students to sit at a table facing the class. Tell the three they're going to be fortune-tellers, and ask them

to choose names for themselves. (You may suggest names such as Madame _____ and Mister _____.) Write these names on cards and prop them up in front of the fortune-tellers. Then give each of the three a hat containing several folded slips of paper bearing phrases like the following.

get married	get divorced	buy a big house
win a bingo game	travel around the world	get a ring
get a raise	get a new job	have a baby
win the lottery	buy a red car	take a vacation in Australia
find $100 on the street	buy lots of new clothes	meet the President
visit your country	speak a lot of English	get a dog
start a business	travel all around the United States	meet someone from your past
get a computer	catch a 30-pound fish	eat bad food and get sick
be on TV	get rich	go to Europe
learn to fix your car	buy a motorcycle	buy an apartment building

Have the class ask questions about themselves using the time expressions on the chalkboard, and have the fortune-tellers pull the answers out of their hats and make them into sentences. Write this sample exchange on the chalkboard.

Minh: Madame Chu, what's going to happen to me next year?

Madame Chu: Minh, you're going to meet the President.

2. To review statement and question formation with *going to*, put these time expressions on the chalkboard: *this weekend, next week, next month, this summer, five years from now*. Put students in pairs and have them interview their partners about what they're going to do at these times. Tell the interviewers to take notes on their partners' plans. Then have each student write a short paragraph on his or her partner's plans for the future and hand it in.

3. Strip Story. Using the dialogues on page 151 of the Student Book as models, type out two new dialogues and cut them into strips of paper, with one strip per line of text. Put students into groups of three and give each group all of the strips necessary to create the two dialogues. (The strips should not be in order.) Ask students to arrange the strips to create two conversations. Then have them practice the conversations aloud.

UNIT 24 EXERCISES

A. Read the notes on Mr. Morgan's desk. Then write sentences about what he is and isn't going to do this week.

Mon., May 5	Tues., May 6	Wed., May 7	Thurs., May 8	Fri., May 9
~~play golf~~	~~go swimming~~	take the kids to the zoo	~~see the dentist~~	~~buy a birthday present for May~~
see the doctor	meet Tom at the airport	run with Tom	take Tom to the airport	meet with new teachers at 3:30

1. _Today, he's going to see the doctor._

   He isn't going to play golf.

2. _Tomorrow,_ _____

   _____

3. _____

   _____

4. _____

   _____

5. _____

   _____

B. Look at the phrases. Write sentences about what you are and aren't going to do this weekend.

1. clean the house _____

2. climb a mountain _____

3. read the paper _____

4. eat out _____

5. relax at home _____

6. ride a horse _____

UNIT 25 Can You Help Me, Please?

Topic: problems at work

Life Skills/Competencies: work schedule changes; requesting assistance

Structure: modal *can*

Vocabulary

I can't open this bottle. It's too tight.	I can open it for you.
I can't understand these directions.	I can explain them to you.
I can't reach that box.	I can get it for you.
I can't move this box. It's too heavy.	I can help you move it.
I can't start this machine.	I can help you start it.
I can't find the sugar.	I can help you find it.

Teaching Suggestions
Activity 1

Refer to the procedure on page v.

If there is any doubt about your students understanding *can/can't*, precede the presentation by writing the two words on the chalkboard and clarifying them with a few easy examples. For example: *Can I speak English?...Yes, I can. Can I touch the ceiling* [attempting to do so]?*...No, I can't.*

Ask questions like the following to present the pictures.

> *What's the problem here?; Why is this person having this problem?;*
>
> *Do you ever have this problem?; What do you do when you have this problem?;*
>
> *What can you say to a friend with this problem?*

The following is a sample presentation of Picture 1 (I can't open this bottle. It's too tight).

> Today we're going to talk about having problems at work and asking for help. Take a look here. What's this woman holding?...Yes, a bottle. And what does she want to do?...Yes, she wants to open the bottle. But can she open the bottle?...No, she can't. Why can't she open the bottle? Is it too big, or too tight [pantomiming trying to open a tightly capped bottle]?...Yes. It's too tight. What else is sometimes too tight?...Is your belt sometimes too tight [pulling belt tight]?...Yes, belts are sometimes too tight. And do you sometimes hold your husband or wife tight [pantomiming this]?...Yes. And what else is sometimes too tight?...Yes, sometimes shoes are too tight [pantomiming]. What else?...Yes, sometimes a jar is too tight, and we can't open it [pantomiming]. Now, back to the picture. This woman can't open the bottle because it's too tight. If your friend at work has this problem, you can say, "I can open it for you." Can you say that? Try it, Heng...Now you try it, Leticia: "I can open it for you."

Activity 2

Refer to the procedure on page vi.

After students have repeated all of the sentences, teach the difference between the pronunciation of *can* and *can't* in statements. Write these sentences on the chalkboard. In each negative statement, put a dot above *can't* and other stressed sylables. In each affirmative statement, cross out the word *can* and above it write *kn*, and put a dot above the main verb, as follows.

I can't open this bottle.   I can open it for you.

I can't understand these directions.   I can explain them for you.

Explain that the difference in the pronunciation of *can* and *can't* in statements isn't the final *t* in *can't*, which is often dropped. What distinguishes the two is the fact that the word *can't* receives stress and the vowel is pronounced fully, while the word *can* is unstressed and the vowel is reduced. Have students repeat these sentences with the correct stress and vowel sounds. Then continue modeling the rest of the sentences on the page and have students repeat as necessary. Go through the sentences a third time, calling out a number and having two students say the corresponding sentences. Correct their pronunciation as necessary.

When students do the pairwork, Student A will read only the problem to cue the picture for Student B to point to.

Grammar Box   (page 155 of Student Book)

Write these cues on the chalkboard: *I can _____ for you* and *I can help you _____*. Ask students to volunteer to help, using the cued sentences, as you dramatize various problems with things in the classroom. For example:

T: (pointing to a book on top of a file cabinet) I can't reach that book.

S: I can get it for you. (pulling the book down and handing it to you)

T: Thanks, Pablo.

T: (attempting to push a heavy desk forward) I can't move this desk.

S: I can help you move it. (coming forward to help move the desk)

T: Thanks, So San.

T: (drawing a Chinese character or a word in some other foreign language on the chalkboard) I can't understand this word.

S: I can explain it for you. It means "horse."

T: Thanks, Menh.

Activity 4

Refer to the procedure on page ix.

After students finish the pairwork, have them continue working with their partners to write two conversations about problems they sometimes encounter at work. After they finish writing, have them practice these conversations aloud and share them with the class.

Activity 5

Ask questions like the following to present the pictures.

What's the problem in this picture?

How does this problem happen?

Does this problem ever happen to you?

Can you (change a tire) ?

What do you use to (change a tire) ?

The following is a sample presentation of Picture 1 (fix a broken dish).

> Today I want to ask you about some little jobs at home—if you can do them or not. Let's take a look at this picture. What's this?...Yes, it's a dish. Where do we use dishes?...Yes, we use dishes in the kitchen. And why do we use dishes?...We use dishes to eat. Now, what happens if we drop a dish [pantomiming this, with the sound of a crash]? Yes, the dish breaks! Do you sometimes break a dish?...I see a lot of you do. Me too! Look at these two pictures [pointing]. Which dish is broken?...Yes, the one on the left is broken. Class, what does "broken" mean?... Yes, "broken" means it breaks. Now let me ask you, Kim, can you fix a broken dish?...You can? Good. Do you fix a broken dish with a hammer [pantomiming]?... No, you don't fix a broken dish with a hammer. You fix a broken dish with...Yes, you fix a broken dish with glue.

After you've presented the pictures, have students work in pairs. One student says the phrases and the other student points to the appropriate pictures while covering up the words.

Grammar Box   (page 156 of Student Book)

Refer to the procedure on page viii.

Ask students a series of yes/no questions about what they can and can't do. This is a good time to review vocabulary relating to sports and leisure activities (e.g., *Can you swim/play volleyball/dance?*) and vocabulary relating to job duties (e.g., *Can you sew clothes/fix cars/drive a bus?*). After several students have given answers, have students ask you several questions about what you can and can't do.

Activity 6

Put the model dialogue on the chalkboard and practice it with the students. Continue asking students if they can fix a leaking faucet until you find two who can and two who can't. Write these dialogues on the board and practice them with the students.

A: Can you fix a leaking faucet?   A: Can you fix a leaking faucet?

B: Yes, I can. What about you?   B: No, I can't. What about you?

A: I can too.   A: I can't either.

Call students' attention to the fact that *I can too* is used when both people can do something and *I can't either* is used when both people can't do it.

Activities 7 and 8

Refer to the procedure on page x.

Prepare students for the activities on page 157 of the Student Book by asking these questions.

How many hours a day do you work?; Do you sometimes work more than 8 hours?;
How many hours of overtime do you work?; Do you get paid more money for working
overtime?; How much more?; Who works the day shift?; Do you sometimes work
a different shift?; Who changes your schedule?

Expansion Activity

Have students do a mingling activity in which they move around the classroom and ask questions of several other students. Pass out copies of (or have students copy from the chalkboard) the following form.

Find 3 people with a washer and dryer.	Find 3 people with a VCR.
1. _____	1. _____
2. _____	2. _____
3. _____	3. _____
Find 3 people with a garage.	Find 3 people with a basement.
1. _____	1. _____
2. _____	2. _____
3. _____	3. _____

Before starting the activity, read the instructions with the students, explaining unfamiliar vocabulary. Next, model the task. Circulate and ask several students if they can play tennis. Write the names of those who can on your form. Then have all students stand up and begin interviewing their classmates.

A. Look at the pictures at the top of page 156. Write sentences about what you can and can't do.

<u>Can</u>   <u>Can't</u>

I can _____   *I can't* _____

_____   _____

_____   _____

_____   _____

_____   _____

B. Complete the conversations.

1. A: I can't **move the desk.** _____

    B: I can help you move it.

2. A: I can't _____

    B: I can get it for you.

3. A: _____

    B: I can help you find it.

4. A: _____

    B: I can fix it for you.

5. A: _____

    B: I can explain them to you.

6. A: _____

    B: I can change it for you.

7. A: _____

    B: I can help you start it.

8. A: _____

    B: I can open it for you.

UNIT 26 Where Did Maria Go Yesterday?

Topic: past events

Life Skills/Competencies: eating out; the calendar

Structure: past tense

Vocabulary   main dishes   side dishes   sandwiches   drinks

Teaching Suggestions

Activity 1

Refer to the procedure on page v.

The places depicted in the calendar have all been previously introduced, so you will use this presentation to introduce the time expressions from page 160 of the Student Book. The tense marker *did* will be used in the presentation but not formally introduced until page 162. Elicit short answers from students, as the irregular form *went* will not be formally introduced until Unit 27.

The following is a sample presentation of August 23, 22, 21, and 20 on the cal‑

> Today we're going to talk about what places Maria went to this month. First, what do we   here?... Yes, it's another calendar. And what month is it?...It's August. And what's the date today [nting to "today" in the calendar]?...Yes, today is August 24th. Now if this is today [pointing again], what day is this [pointing to Aug. 23]?...Yes, it's yesterday. And where did Maria go yesterday?...Yes, s e went to a restaurant yesterday. Now, if this is yesterday [pointing again], then what day is this [pointing to Aug. 22]?...Yes. It's the day before yesterday. And where did Maria go the day before yesterday?...Yes, she went to the bank the day before yesterday. Now, [pointing to Aug. 21], how many days ago was this day [counting backward from Aug. 24]?...Yes, it was three days ago. And this day [pointing to Aug. 20]?...Four days ago. And what about this [pointing to Aug. 17]?...Yes. That was one week ago. Now [directing attention away from picture] what time was it one hour ago [looking at watch]?...Yes, one hour ago it was 2:15. And what year was it ten years ago?...Very good, ten years ago it was 1985. Now [directing attention back to picture and pointing to Aug. 21] where did Maria go three days ago?...Yes, three days ago she went to the hospital. And what about four days ago?

Activity 3

Refer to the procedure on page vii.

After students finish the Listen and Write activity, have them close their books and look at a large calendar at the front of the classroom. Ask them to tell you the current day, month, and date. Then reinforce the past time expressions by pointing to various past dates and asking three students where they went at that time. Have them respond with short answers. For example:

> T: Ali, where did you go the day before yesterday?
>
> A: To work.

Grammar Box   (page 162 of Student Book)

Refer to the procedure on page viii.

Refer to a current calendar. Point to various past times on the calendar and ask individual students where they went on that day. Have half of the class transform your questions into the third-person singular and the other half of the class repeat the answers. For example:

T: (pointing to yesterday) Where did you go last Sunday, Yun?

Y: Downtown.

Ss1: Where did he go last Sunday?

Ss2: Downtown.

Activity 7

As you practice the conversations with the students, teach them the pronunciation of *did you* in informal speech. Write the two questions on the chalkboard, crossing out the words *did you* and above them writing *dija*, as follows.

> Where ~~did you~~ go last Sunday?
>   *dija*
>
> Where ~~did you~~ go last summer?
>   *dija*

Explain that this is often the pronunciation of *did you* in spoken English. Have students repeat the sentences using *dija*. Next, refer to a current calendar. As you point to various past times, have students ask questions with *dija* about where you went at those times. Respond with short answers.

Activity 8

Prepare students for the activities on pages 163 and 164 of the Student Book by asking these questions.

> *Do you eat in restaurants?; How often?; Who do you eat with?;*
>
> *What kind of restaurants do you go to?; What kind of food do you order?*

To introduce the vocabulary items on the menu, bring in pictures of the foods or make simple sketches on the chalkboard. Discuss each item by asking students how much it costs, if they like it, and when they eat it—for breakfast, lunch, or dinner.

Activity 9

After students finish the pairwork, have several pairs perform their dialogues for the class.

After practicing the conversation at the bottom of the page, ask students who pays for the meal when couples or groups of people go out to eat in their countries.

Activity 11

Before students start the pairwork, have them ask you the six questions. Respond by offering information about a recent experience you had at a restaurant.

After students finish the writing task, ask several of them questions about their partners' experiences at restaurants.

For reinforcement of language used in restaurants, refer to Expansion Activities 1 and 2.

Expansion Activities

1. Make photocopies of a menu from a fast food restaurant and pass them out in class. Have students repeat the menu items after you, and teach any unfamiliar vocabulary. Ask students how much each item costs and if they like it or not. Then put students in pairs and have them make dialogues following the model on page 163 of the Student Book. After both students have had several chances to practice ordering a meal, ask several pairs of students to perform one conversation for the class.

2. Initiate a class discussion on the social etiquette practiced in restaurants in students' countries and in the United States. Ask these questions.

How do you call over a waiter or waitress in your country?;

How do you ask for the check in your country?;

Do you tip waiters and waitresses in your country? How much?

During the course of the discussion, explain restaurant etiquette in the United States. To summon a waiter, you raise your hand above your head and shake it gently to catch the waiter's eye. You request the check by raising your hand above your head and, after catching the waiter's eye, turning your hand over and making a writing gesture in the air. The standard tip is 15 percent.

A. **Make a calendar for this month. Write the name of the month and number the days.**

SUN.	MON.	TUES.	WED.	THURS.	FRI.	SAT.

Now write the dates.

1. yesterday _____

2. five days ago _____

3. last Friday _____

4. the day before yesterday _____

5. two weeks ago _____

6. last week _____

7. one week ago Sunday _____

8. last Wednesday _____

B. **Complete the conversation.**

A: _____ did you go last night?

B: To the movies.

A: Oh, really? _____ movie did you see?

B: *Vacation in Vienna.*

A: Hmm. _____ did you go_____?

B: Tony and Jane.

A: _____ did you get there?

B: By car.

A: _____ _____ did it cost?

B: $7.00.

A: _____ did you get home?

B: At midnight.

UNIT 27 | *What Did John Do Last Week?*

Topic: past events

Life Skill/Competency: calling in sick

St 1 ructure: past tense

Vocabulary

cough all day	cry	miss work
call in sick	stay home	play with the kids
rest in bed	wash (her) hair	bark at the mail carrier
argue	dance all night	didn't do anything

Teaching Suggestions
Activity 1

Refer to the procedure on page v.

You will use the past tense *-ed* in your presentation, but students will not produce it until it is formally introduced on page 167 of the Student Book.

Ask questions like the following to present the pictures.

What did ___(John)___ do on ___(Tuesday)___?

Why did he/she/they _(cough all day)_? (free speculation)

Do/Did you ever ___(argue)___?

How often do you ___(cry)___?

When did you ___(cry)___?

Do you like to _(rest in bed)_?

The following is a sample presentation of Pictures 1 and 2 (what John did last week).

> Today we're going to talk about what people did last week. First let's look at John. What did he do last Tuesday? Remember this picture?...Yes, he coughed. In the morning? In the afternoon? When [indicating the sun]?...Yes, he coughed all day. It wasn't a good day for John. And what did he do on Wednesday? Did he go to work, or did he call in sick?...Yes, he called in sick. What does that mean, "called in sick"?...Yes, he called his work. And what did he say?...Yes. He said he wasn't going to work that day because he was sick. Do you ever call in sick?...You do? When did you call in sick, Luisa?... Oh, you called in sick last Wednesday. So that's why you weren't in school! And did your boss get angry when you called in sick?...No? Well, you must have a nice boss. Now let's look at what John did on Thursday.

Activity 3

If students need more practice forming the past tense of verbs, write these verbs on the chalkboard and have students write them in the past tense.

wait	nap	yawn	hurry	bark
exercise	watch	pray	kiss	start
scratch	raise	shave	work	jog

In addition, teach students when to use the long and short endings on past tense verbs. First, say these pairs of verbs aloud, clapping out the syllables: *clean/cleaned, brush/brushed, wait/waited,* and *add/added.* Go through the pairs of verbs again, having students clap and repeat after you. Then write *Long sound* and *Short sound* at the top of two columns on one side of the chalkboard and the following list of verbs on the other side of the chalkboard.

| look | study | start | live | add | watch | visit | cry |
| end | comb | repeat | lower | shave | work | wait | |

Point to the verbs one by one and say both the simple and past tense forms. Have students tell you whether both forms of the verb have the same number of syllables or whether the past tense form has an extra syllable. Write each verb in the appropriate column. Then circle the verb endings that require an additional syllable: *t* and *d*. Explain that when verbs end with /t/ and /d/, the past tense form will have an additional syllable. Point to the verbs again and have students say the past tense of each one.

Grammar Box   (page 168 of Student Book)

Refer to the procedure on page viii.

Refer to a current calendar. Point to various past times on the calendar and ask individuals and pairs of students yes/no questions about their activities on those days. Wait for an affirmative response. Then have half of the class ask the corresponding *Wh-* question and the other half of the class give the answer. For example,

> T: (pointing to the day before yesterday) Did you work
> the day before yesterday, Ana?
>
> A: Yes.
>
> Ss1: What did she do the day before yesterday?
>
> Ss2: She worked.

Appropriate verb phrases for this activity include *work, stay home, study, cook a meal, wash the dishes, watch TV, exercise, play cards/tennis/baseball/soccer.*

Activity 5

Refer to the procedure on page ix.

After students finish the pairwork, have them look at page 165 of the Student Book and write three sentences about each character or pair of characters. For example:

> On Tuesday, John coughed all day.
>
> On Wednesday, he called in sick.
>
> On Thursday, he rested in bed.

Activities 6 and 7

Refer to the procedure on page x.

Prepare students for the conversation and the activities on pages 168 and 169 of the Student Book by asking these questions.

> *When you're sick, do you go to work?; What do you do?; Who do you call?*

Activity 8

For reinforcement of language related to calling in sick, refer to Expansion Activity 1.

Grammar Box   (page 170 of Student Book)

Refer to the procedure on page viii.

Have students practice using these irregular verbs in sentences. Ask questions about the present, the past, and habits. For example:

> T: Joni, how are you today?
>
> J: I'm fine.
>
> T: How were you at 11:30 last night?
>
> J: I was tired.

T: Marco, what do you usually eat for breakfast?

M: I usually eat bread.

T: What did you eat this morning?

M: I ate bread.

Activity 10

After students finish the writing task, have them read their paragraphs aloud to their partners.

For reinforcement of past tense verbs, refer to Expansion Activities 2 and 3.

Expansion Activities

1. Strip Story. Using the dialogue at the bottom of page 168 of the Student Book as a model, type out a new dialogue and cut it into strips of paper, with one strip per line of text. Put students into groups of three and give each group all of the strips necessary to create the dialogue. (The strips should not be in order.) Have them work together to put the strips in the correct order. Then have them practice the conversation aloud.

2. To review the formation of familiar regular and irregular verbs in the past tense, write two questions on the chalkboard: *Where did he/she go?* and *What did he/she do?* Give each student a flashcard (which you have made before class) with two commands. For example:

    Go to the window. Open it.

    Go to the table at the front of the room. Move it.

    Go to the door. Close it.

    Go to the chalkboard. Erase it.

    Go to the corner of the room. Rub your neck.

    Go to the back of the room. Touch your toes.

    Go to the map. Point to China.

    Go to front of the room. Scratch your head.

    Call on individuals to perform the actions and then return to their seats. Then have half of the class ask two questions and the other half respond. For example:

    Ss1: Where did he go?

    Ss2: He went to the window.

    Ss1: What did he do?

    Ss2: He opened it.

3. Write *Yesterday after class* on the chalkboard and dictate the following short paragraph for students to write in their notebooks.

    Yesterday after class, I went home. I was hungry. I cooked dinner for my family. We ate fish. It was good. After dinner, I washed the dishes. Next we watched a video on TV. It was good too. Then I was tired. I went to bed at 11:00.

    After checking students' work, have them write a short paragraph about their activities the previous day. To steer students away from using unfamiliar irregular verbs, you may put a list of familiar regular and irregular verbs on the chalkboard and suggest that students choose verbs from this list.

A. **Complete the story about Maria. Write the past tense of the words in the box. Use each word once.**

argue	call	cry	eat	fill
go	have	is	wait	walk

Last Tuesday, Maria had a bad day. In the morning, she missed the 7:30 bus. She _____ twenty minutes for the next bus. She _____ late to work.

At work, she _____ out forms and did some work for Mr. Morgan. She _____ a sandwich for lunch. It wasn't very good. So she _____ a stomachache all afternoon.

After work, Maria _____ to Stan's apartment. Stan wasn't there. So Maria _____ home to her apartment. Stan _____ on the telephone an hour later. They _____ on the phone. That night, Maria _____ and didn't sleep. It was a terrible day!

B. **Read the answers and complete the questions.**

1. Where ____*do you go*____ most summers?

    Most summers, I go to the beach.

2. Where _____ last summer?

    Last summer, I went to Hong Kong.

3. Where _____ this summer?

    This summer, I'm going camping in the mountains.

4. What _____ most evenings?

    Most evenings, I read the newspaper.

5. What _____ yesterday evening?

    Yesterday evening, I saw a movie.

6. What _____ this evening?

    This evening, I'm going to visit my parents.